WILLIAMS-SONOMA

FISH

RECIPES AND TEXT
SHIRLEY KING

GENERAL EDITOR
CHUCK WILLIAMS

PHOTOGRAPHS
NOEL BARNHURST

SIMON & SCHUSTER • **SOURCE**

NEW YORK • LONDON • TORONTO • SYDNEY • SINGAPORE

CONTENTS

ON THE GRILL

HEARTY DISHES

SHELLFISH

INTRODUCTION

Today, everyone's looking for ways to eat more healthfully. One of the easiest and most appealing ways to do so is to eat fish. Not only are many fish naturally lean, but it seems that medical research is constantly uncovering nutritional benefits in seafood. Plus, fish figures in just about every cuisine around the world, which means there are endlessly interesting ways to prepare the many types of fish available.

In this cookbook, we've aimed to offer recipes for a wide range of fish. There's even a section on other types of seafood, including crab, shrimp, mussels, and lobster. Alongside every recipe is an informative side note that demystifies a technique or ingredient used in the recipe. Remembering that the end result of cooking is only as good as the ingredients that go into it, you can look to the chapter of basics at the back of the book to learn about how to select the very best and freshest fish and seafood. Then turn to any recipe in this cookbook, and enjoy.

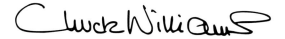

THE CLASSICS

The recipes in this chapter stem from very different culinary traditions around the world but have become familiar favorites because of their broad appeal. Some are quick and simple to prepare, others are more a labor of love—but all are delicious additions to a cook's repertoire of recipes.

FILLETS OF SOLE MEUNIÈRE

To prevent the fillets from curling up while cooking, score the skin side with 2 shallow crisscross cuts (see Note).

Put the flour in a shallow bowl and stir in 1 tablespoon salt and ½ teaspoon white pepper. Sprinkle both sides of each fillet lightly with salt and white pepper. Dredge them in the seasoned flour.

Heat a large sauté pan over medium-high heat, then add 2 teaspoons of the butter with 2 teaspoons of the oil. When the butter foam begins to subside, shake the excess flour from 2 of the fillets and put them in the pan, skin side up. Reduce the heat to medium and cook until golden on the bottom, about 1 minute. Using a wide spatula, carefully turn the fillets over and cook until golden on the second side and opaque throughout, about 2 minutes longer, depending on their thickness.

Place the fillets on warmed individual plates or a platter and cover loosely with aluminum foil to keep warm. Wipe the sauté pan clean with paper towels and repeat to cook the remaining fillets in 2 batches.

When all of the fillets have been cooked, clean the pan again. To make the sauce, melt the remaining 4 tablespoons (2 fl oz/60 ml) butter over medium heat, add the lemon juice, and swirl the mixture in the pan. Pour over the warm fillets. Sprinkle with the parsley, garnish with the lemon wedges and parsley sprigs, and serve immediately.

Note: To identify the skin side, look for thin silver-whitish remnants of skin on one side of each fillet.

Variation Tip: Fillets of flounder, lemon sole, or gray sole can also be used in place of the sole in this recipe.

MAKES 4–6 SERVINGS

6 sole fillets, 6–8 oz (185–250 g) each, skinned

1 cup (5 oz/155 g) all-purpose (plain) flour

Coarse salt and freshly ground white pepper

6 tablespoons (3 oz/90 g) unsalted butter

6 teaspoons olive oil or canola oil

¼ cup (2 fl oz/60 ml) fresh lemon juice, plus 1 lemon, cut into wedges

1 tablespoon minced fresh flat-leaf (Italian) parsley

4 fresh flat-leaf (Italian) parsley or chervil sprigs

TROUT AMANDINE

¾ cup (3 oz/90 g) sliced
(flaked) almonds

4 trout fillets, 5–7 oz
(155–220 g) each,
with skin intact

1 cup (5 oz/155 g)
all-purpose (plain) flour

2 tablespoons sweet
paprika

Coarse salt and freshly
ground pepper

4 tablespoons (2 oz/60 g)
unsalted butter

4 tablespoons (2 fl oz/
60 ml) olive oil

2 tablespoons fresh
lemon juice

2 teaspoons
Worcestershire sauce

Chopped fresh flat-leaf
(Italian) parsley for garnish

Preheat the oven to 400°F (200°C). Spread the almonds in a baking pan and toast until they turn light golden, about 5 minutes. Remove from the oven and transfer to a plate. Set aside.

To prevent the fillets from curling up while cooking, score the skin side (see Note, page 10) with 2 shallow crisscross cuts.

In a shallow bowl, combine the flour, paprika, 1 tablespoon salt, and 1 teaspoon pepper. Stir with a fork to blend well. Dredge the fillets in the seasoned flour.

Heat a large sauté pan over medium-high heat, then add 1 table-spoon of the butter with 1 tablespoon of the oil. When the butter foam begins to subside, shake the excess flour from 2 of the fillets and put them in the pan, skin side up. Sauté until they are golden on the bottom, about 1 minute. Using a wide spatula, carefully turn the fillets and cook until golden on the other side and opaque throughout, about 2 minutes. Place the fish on a warmed platter and cover loosely with foil to keep warm. Wipe the pan clean with paper towels and repeat to cook the remaining fillets.

When all the fillets have been cooked, clean the pan again. Over medium heat, melt the remaining 2 tablespoons butter with the remaining 2 tablespoons oil. When the butter foam subsides, add the almonds and sauté for 30 seconds, then add the lemon juice, Worcestershire sauce, and a pinch of salt. Swirl the sauce around in the pan and pour over the trout fillets. Garnish with the parsley and serve immediately.

MAKES 4 SERVINGS

DREDGING

Dredging fish fillets in flour slows the escape of moisture during cooking and promotes good color and crispness. To dredge, drag each side of a fillet through the flour, coating it completely, and shake off the excess. Dredge just a few minutes before sautéing so that the flour coating does not draw moisture from the fish and become gummy.

NEW ENGLAND FISH CHOWDER

In a soup pot, heat the oil over medium heat. Add the bacon and fry until crisp, about 5 minutes. Using a slotted spoon, transfer to paper towels to drain. Pour off all but 2 tablespoons of the fat from the pot. Add the onion and the garlic, if using, and sauté until soft, about 5 minutes.

Stir in the flour and cook for 30 seconds. Pour in the half-and-half, milk, and fish stock and bring slowly to a boil. Reduce the heat to low and stir in the cornstarch mixture, mixing well. Simmer for 1 minute. Season to taste with salt and pepper.

Add the potatoes and simmer uncovered, stirring occasionally, until they are nearly tender, about 10 minutes. Add the cod and bacon and cook until the fish is opaque throughout, another 4 minutes.

Ladle the chowder into warmed soup bowls and garnish with the parsley. Serve immediately.

Variation Tip: Other fish and shellfish, such as haddock, red snapper, mahimahi, monkfish, littleneck clams, mussels, or shucked oysters, can be used in place of or in addition to the cod.

MAKES 4 SERVINGS

POTATO TYPES

Yukon gold potatoes are an excellent choice for this recipe because of their buttery taste and firm texture. Classified as all-purpose potatoes, they are lower in starch than russets and hold their shape well during cooking. Other lower-starch, or waxy, potatoes that would substitute well are red or white potatoes. Russet potatoes, which are high in starch, are best reserved for baking, mashing, or making French fries (page 21).

1 tablespoon canola or safflower oil

6 slices bacon, finely chopped

1 yellow onion, finely chopped

4 cloves garlic, minced (optional)

3 tablespoons all-purpose (plain) flour

1 cup (8 fl oz/250 ml) half-and-half (half cream)

1½ cups (12 fl oz/375 ml) milk

2 cups (16 fl oz/500 ml) fish stock (page 110) or bottled clam juice

1 tablespoon cornstarch (cornflour), dissolved in ½ cup (4 fl oz/125 ml) cold water

Coarse salt and freshly ground pepper

4 Yukon gold potatoes, ¾ lb (375 g) total, peeled and cut into ½-inch (12-mm) dice

1 cod fillet, 1 lb (500 g), pin bones removed, cut into 1-inch (2.5-cm) cubes

1 tablespoon minced fresh flat-leaf (Italian) parsley

BOUILLABAISSE

¾ lb (375 g) mixed firm fillets such as striped bass, halibut, monkfish, or mahimahi

¾ lb (375 g) mixed fish steaks such as red snapper, rockfish, cod, or black cod

¼ cup (2 fl oz/60 ml) olive oil

3 yellow onions, chopped

1 carrot, peeled and grated

8 cloves garlic, minced

2 leeks, including tender green parts, chopped

1 fennel bulb, trimmed and cut into small dice

4 tomatoes, peeled, seeded, and chopped (page 86)

Zests of 1 orange and 1 lemon, removed in wide ribbons with a peeler

1 teaspoon saffron threads

1 bouquet garni *(far right)*

8 cups (64 fl oz/2 l) fish stock (page 110) or clam juice

¾ lb (375 g) shrimp, peeled and deveined

1 lb (500 g) mussels, scrubbed and debearded

Salt and ground pepper

1 baguette, cut into thin slices and lightly toasted

Rouille for serving (page 90)

Remove any pin bones from the fillets. Cut the fillets and the steaks crosswise into pieces 1½ inches (4 cm) wide. Set aside.

In a soup pot, heat 2 tablespoons of the olive oil over medium-high heat. Add the onions and carrot, reduce the heat to medium, and cook, stirring frequently, until the onions are soft and starting to turn golden, about 6 minutes. Add the garlic, leeks, and fennel and cook until the fennel is soft, 5 minutes. Add the tomatoes and orange and lemon zests and cook for 10 minutes longer. Add the saffron, the bouquet garni, and the fish stock. Raise the heat to high and bring to a boil. Add the remaining 2 tablespoons olive oil and boil vigorously for 15 minutes to blend the flavors.

Reduce the heat to medium and add the fish fillets, shrimp, and mussels, discarding any that do not close to the touch. Cook until the mussels start to open, about 3 minutes longer. Add the fish steaks and cook until the fish is opaque throughout, about 3 minutes more. Discard any mussels that have not opened. Season to taste with salt and pepper.

Ladle the soup into warmed serving bowls. Spread the toasted baguette slices with rouille and use to garnish the soup or serve them alongside.

Note: This famous fish soup is a signature dish of Marseilles, in the south of France, and the fish suggested here are good substitutes for the usual French ones. In Marseilles, bouillabaisse broth is traditionally strained and served first with croutons and rouille (a thick garlic and red-pepper sauce). The shrimp, fish, and mussels are then served as a second course.

MAKES 6–8 SERVINGS

BOUQUET GARNI

A bouquet garni, used for seasoning soups, stews, and braises, classically consists of a few parsley sprigs with stems, thyme sprigs, and bay leaves. Sometimes peppercorns and whole garlic cloves are added for extra flavor. For this recipe, tie 3 fresh flat-leaf (Italian) parsley sprigs, 2 fresh thyme sprigs, and 3 bay leaves together in a small square of cheesecloth (muslin). The herbs are tied in cheesecloth so that they can be easily removed from the soup before serving.

OVEN-POACHED WHOLE SALMON

Preheat the oven to 425°F (220°C). Rinse out the fish. Spread out a double layer of heavy aluminum foil large enough to enclose the fish with some overlap. Place the fish on the foil and rub olive oil over the outside of the fish. Sprinkle with salt inside and out. Halve 1 of the lemons and squeeze the juice all over the fish. Slice the remaining lemon and put the slices and the dill inside the fish.

Fold the foil lengthwise around the fish and tuck in the ends of the foil. Use another sheet of foil to wrap the fish securely. Place the wrapped fish diagonally on a rimmed baking sheet. Pour water to a depth of ⅛ inch (3 mm) into the baking sheet. Slide the fish into the oven with its head pointing toward one of the back corners.

Cook until an instant-read thermometer inserted into the thickest part of the fish, behind the head, registers 140°F (60°C), about 40 minutes for a 6-lb (3-kg) fish or 1 hour for a 9-lb (4.5-kg) fish.

Meanwhile, prepare the sauce: In a blender or food processor, combine the mayonnaise, lemon juice, garlic, and spinach and blend until smooth. Add the parsley, basil, mint, and chives and blend until almost smooth. Season to taste with salt and pepper.

Remove the fish from the oven. Unwrap the foil from the head and pour any accumulated juices into a bowl. Let the fish cool, then unwrap it carefully. With a knife, loosen the skin behind the head and along the back and belly, then roll back the skin to remove it. Using 2 wide spatulas, transfer the fish to a serving platter.

Dip the cucumber slices in the reserved fish juices and overlap on the fish to mimic scales. Dip tarragon leaves and arrange to look like the bones of the fish. Alternate the lemon slices and parsley sprigs around the sides of the fish. Serve with the sauce alongside.

MAKES 8–12 SERVINGS

1 whole salmon, 6–9 lb (3–4.5 kg), cleaned by the fishmonger

2 tablespoons olive oil

Coarse salt

2 lemons

1 bunch fresh dill, stemmed

FOR THE SAUCE:

1 cup (8 fl oz/250 ml) mayonnaise

2 tablespoons lemon juice

1 clove garlic

1 lb (500 g) spinach, stemmed

1 bunch *each* fresh flat-leaf (Italian) parsley, fresh basil, and fresh mint, stemmed

1 bunch fresh chives

Coarse salt and pepper

FOR THE GARNISH:

1 English (hothouse) cucumber, cut into slices 1/16 inch (2 mm) thick (page 78)

1 bunch fresh tarragon, stemmed

1 lemon, thinly sliced

1 bunch fresh curly-leaf or flat-leaf (Italian) parsley, stemmed

FISH AND CHIPS

FOR THE BATTER:

**1 cup (5 oz/155 g)
all-purpose (plain) flour**

½ teaspoon baking powder

**Coarse salt and freshly
ground pepper**

1 cup (8 fl oz/250 ml) beer

1 egg, separated

FOR THE CHIPS:

**4 large russet potatoes,
about ½ lb (250 g) each**

**Canola or corn oil for
deep-frying**

**4 pieces cod fillet, each
¾ inch (2 cm) thick, about
1½ lb (750 g) total weight,
pin bones removed**

Coarse salt and pepper

**1 cup (8 fl oz/250 ml)
mayonnaise**

**1 teaspoon minced garlic or
snipped fresh chives**

1 tablespoon Dijon mustard

1 lemon, sliced into wedges

**4 fresh flat-leaf (Italian)
parsley sprigs for garnish**

**Ketchup for serving
(optional)**

**Malt vinegar for serving
(optional)**

To start the batter, in a bowl, combine the flour, baking powder, ½ teaspoon salt, and ¼ teaspoon pepper. Pour the beer into another bowl and whisk in the egg yolk. Make a well in the center of the flour mixture. Gradually whisk the beer mixture into the flour mixture until a smooth batter forms. Set aside.

To make the chips, peel and cut the potatoes into slices ⅓ inch (9 mm) thick and then into sticks ⅓ inch (9 mm) wide. Spread on paper towels. Do not rinse.

Position a rack in the upper third of the oven and a rack in the lower third of the oven. Preheat the oven to 450°F (230°C). Pour the oil to a depth of 3 inches (7.5 cm) into a Dutch oven or deep fryer and heat over high heat to 365°F (185°C). Add the potatoes in batches and fry until they begin to turn golden, about 5 minutes. Using a slotted spoon, transfer to paper towels to drain. Turn off the heat under the oil. In a baking pan, spread the potatoes in a single layer. Bake on the top rack of the oven until crisp, about 5 minutes. Lower the oven temperature to 200°F (95°C).

Meanwhile, pat the fillets dry and season with salt and pepper. In a small bowl, whisk the egg white until soft peaks form; fold into the batter. Over high heat, bring the oil back to 365°F (185°C). Dip 2 fillets into the batter, allowing the excess to drip off. Lower them into the oil. Fry, turning occasionally, until golden, about 5 minutes. Transfer the fish to an ovenproof platter and place on the lower oven rack. Repeat to fry the remaining fish.

In a small bowl, mix the mayonnaise, garlic, and mustard together. Remove the potatoes and fish from the oven. Sprinkle the potatoes with salt and pile them on the platter with the fish. Garnish with lemon wedges and parsley sprigs. Serve with the flavored mayonnaise and ketchup and/or malt vinegar, if you like.

MAKES 4 SERVINGS

DEEP-FRYING

For perfectly crisp and golden deep-fried food, it is essential to maintain the oil at the correct temperature. Use a deep-frying thermometer and adjust the heat to make sure that the temperature does not dip below 350°F (180°C), which would cause the food to absorb oil and become greasy, or rise above 375°F (190°C), which would over-cook the food on the outside without fully cooking the inside. Caution: Do not let the oil reach 400°F (200°C) or above, or it may burst into flames. Use a skimmer or tongs to lower food into hot oil without spattering.

GRAVLAX

In a bowl, mix together the sugar, kosher salt, and 1½ teaspoons black pepper. Line a piece of heavy aluminum foil 20 inches (50 cm) long with plastic wrap. Lay the salmon fillets next to each other on the foil, skin side down and backs touching (the back of each fillet will have thicker flesh than the belly). Spread the sugar-and-salt mixture over the fillets. Sprinkle with the orange and lemon zests, the coarsely chopped dill, and the juniper berries, if using. Fold the foil in half, closing it like a book and pressing the flesh sides of the fillets together. Wrap the foil tightly around the salmon and place the packet in a baking pan. Weight the salmon with a heavy object such as a large can of tomatoes or a foil-wrapped brick. Refrigerate for 3 days, turning the packet over every day. If moisture seeps out, drain it away.

To make the sauce, put the honey mustard and balsamic vinegar in a bowl and whisk to blend. Gradually whisk in the oil in a fine stream to make an emulsion (page 37). Using a spoon, stir in the water, white pepper to taste, and the minced dill.

To serve, unwrap the gravlax and scrape off most of the zest and dill. Using a very sharp slicing knife, cut thin slices on a diagonal across the fish. Serve with the sauce.

Preparation Tips: The salmon should cure for 3 days before being served. Unwrap the salmon and rewrap in fresh plastic wrap. Place in self-sealing plastic bags. Serve now, refrigerate for up to 5 days, or freeze for up to 6 weeks.

Serving Tip: It is easy to carve the gravlax into thin slices when it is partially frozen. Small squares of thinly sliced brown bread such as dark rye or pumpernickel are traditional accompaniments.

MAKES 10–12 APPETIZER SERVINGS

¾ cup (6 oz/185 g) sugar

¾ cup (6 oz/185 g) kosher salt

Freshly ground black pepper

2 same-size center-cut salmon fillets, 1½ lb (750 g) each, with skin intact, pin bones removed

Zests of ½ orange and ½ lemon, removed in wide ribbons with a peeler, cut into thin julienne strips

½ bunch fresh dill, stemmed and coarsely chopped

2 tablespoons juniper berries, crushed (optional)

FOR THE SAUCE:

1 cup (8 oz/250 g) honey mustard

2 tablespoons balsamic vinegar

¾ cup (6 fl oz/180 ml) olive oil

1 tablespoon water

Ground white pepper

2 tablespoons minced fresh dill

SIMPLE SUPPERS

Fish takes only a short time to cook, and after a long day, these recipes can be prepared in just a few minutes without a lot of fuss. And because fish can be prepared in so many different ways and paired with so many different ingredients, these quick and easy recipes provide an opportunity for delicious variety as well.

PAN-ROASTED SALMON FILLETS
IN MANGO JUICE

Lay the salmon fillets in a baking dish in a single layer, skin side up. Pour the mango juice evenly over them. Let stand at room temperature for 20 minutes (but no longer).

Preheat the oven to 450°F (230°C). Drain the fillets, reserving the mango juice, and pat dry.

In a large ovenproof nonstick sauté pan, heat the olive oil over high heat. Add the fillets, skin side down. Reduce the heat to medium and cook until the skin is very crisp, about 5 minutes.

Transfer the sauté pan to the oven and bake the fillets until the flesh is opaque on the outside but still slightly translucent in the center, 2–3 minutes. Remove from the oven and transfer to a warmed platter. Cover loosely with aluminum foil to keep warm.

Pour the reserved mango juice into a small saucepan, bring to a boil, and simmer until thickened, about 5 minutes. Whisk and pour the sauce over the salmon fillets. Garnish with the chives and serve at once.

Note: Be sure to use a nonstick sauté pan to cook the salmon, or the skin will stick to the pan.

Variation Tips: Other firm-fleshed fillets, such as striped bass, black cod, red snapper, rockfish, tilefish, or arctic char, can be used in place of the salmon.

MAKES 4 SERVINGS

4 salmon fillets, 6–8 oz (185–250 g) each, with skin intact, pin bones removed

1¼ cups (10 fl oz/310 ml) mango juice

2 tablespoons olive oil

2 tablespoons minced fresh chives or 1 green (spring) onion, including tender green parts, finely chopped

MAKING MANGO JUICE
If you cannot find bottled mango juice for this quick meal, substitute a peeled ripe mango puréed in a blender with ¾ cup (6 fl oz/180 ml) water. To cut a mango into cubes for puréeing, halve the mango lengthwise to one side of the pit, then cut the pit away from the other half. Make diagonal cuts in the flesh of each half about ¾ inch (2 cm) apart in a crisscross pattern. Using your thumbs, turn the mango half inside out and slice the flesh away from the skin.

BROILED RED SNAPPER WITH ROSEMARY

4 red snapper fillets, 6–8 oz (185–250 g) each, skin and pin bones removed

20 small fresh rosemary sprigs, plus 6 long, leafy rosemary branches, soaked in water for 10 minutes

Dry white wine or water as needed

1 tablespoon olive oil

Coarse salt and freshly ground pepper

¼ cup (2 fl oz / 60 ml) Pernod or Cognac

Preheat the broiler (grill). To prevent the red snapper fillets from curling up while they are cooking, score the skin side (see Note, page 10) with 2 shallow crisscross cuts. Stick the flesh side of each fillet with 5 small rosemary sprigs.

Pour wine into a shallow baking pan to a depth of ⅛ inch (3 mm). Strew the rosemary branches in the pan and place the fillets, flesh side up, on top of the branches. Brush the fillets lightly with the olive oil and sprinkle to taste with salt and pepper.

Broil the fish as close as possible to the heating element until lightly browned on the outside and opaque throughout, 4–7 minutes. With a wide spatula, transfer the fish to a flameproof gratin pan and place the pan over medium heat on the stove top.

To flambé the fish *(right)*, in a small saucepan, heat the Pernod over medium heat until it is hot but not boiling. Completely remove both the saucepan and the pan with the fish from the heat. Pour the warmed liqueur over the fish and ignite the fumes with a long match. When the flames subside, serve the fish immediately with any pan juices poured over the top. If the liqueur does not light, continue to cook until the aroma of the alcohol dissipates.

Note: Flambéed Pernod adds an especially pleasant flavor to fish. Pernod and Ricard are trade names of pastis, the anise-flavored liqueur popular in the south of France.

Variation Tip: Shad, halibut, salmon, arctic char, and baby coho salmon fillets can also be used in place of the red snapper.

MAKES 4 SERVINGS

FLAMBÉING

When flambéing, both the food and the liquor must be warmed. When both are warmed, completely remove the pan of liquor and the pan of food from the stove top. Pour the warmed liquor over the fish and carefully set the liquor's fumes aflame by holding a lit long match just above the fish. Keep hair and loose clothing away from the fire and have a pan lid handy in case the flames grow dangerously high.

HALIBUT FILLET EN PAPILLOTE

BAKING IN PARCHMENT

Parchment (baking) paper is useful for lining pans for nonstick cooking and baking. It comes in a roll and is available in most supermarkets. Cooking in a parchment paper packet—*en papillote*—is a perfect way to steam fish and vegetables for a complete meal. The paper keeps the moisture in, and when the package is opened, the aroma billows out. A baking sheet is the only pan needed, so there is little washing up.

Preheat the oven to 425°F (220°C). Cut a 16-by-20-inch (40-by-50-cm) length of parchment (baking) paper and fold it in half lengthwise. Draw half a heart as large as the paper, beginning at the fold, and cut it out with scissors. Repeat to make 3 more hearts.

In a small bowl, mix together the lime juice, green onion, garlic, jalapeño, and salt and pepper to taste. Sprinkle the fish with the lime juice mixture. In a medium bowl, mix together the carrot, leeks, celery, and parsley.

Spread a paper heart open. Sprinkle a few drops of melted butter in the center of the right-hand side of the heart. Lay 1 fish fillet on the butter and place one-fourth of the vegetables on top. Sprinkle with salt and pepper to taste, more melted butter, and 1 tablespoon of the wine. Brush the inside edge of the paper heart shape with egg white. Fold the paper over and press the edges together. Starting from the top of the heart, fold the edges over twice, working your way along the paper's edge to end with a twist at the bottom of the heart (tuck the twist underneath the packet). Repeat to make 3 more packages. Place the packages on a baking sheet.

Bake until the paper is nicely puffed up and starting to brown, about 20 minutes. Remove from the oven and transfer to warmed plates. Open the packages carefully with scissors and serve at once.

Variation Tip: Fillets of trout, baby coho salmon, red snapper, or salmon can be used instead of the halibut.

MAKES 4 SERVINGS

2 tablespoons fresh lime juice

1 green (spring) onion, including tender green parts, thinly sliced

2 cloves garlic, minced

1 small jalapeño chile, seeded and minced

Coarse salt and freshly ground pepper

4 halibut fillets, each 6–8 oz (185–250 g) and 1 inch (2.5 cm) thick, pin bones removed

1 large carrot, peeled and coarsely grated

2 leeks, white and tender green parts, cut into fine julienne 3 inches (7.5 cm) long

2 celery stalks, cut into fine julienne 3 inches (7.5 cm) long

2 tablespoons chopped fresh flat-leaf (Italian) parsley

4 tablespoons (2 oz/60 g) unsalted butter, melted, or olive oil

4 tablespoons (2 fl oz/60 ml) dry white wine

1 egg white, lightly beaten

COD BAKED WITH SQUASH AND TOMATO

4 Yukon gold potatoes,
1 lb (500 g) total weight

2 tablespoons olive oil or
canola oil

2 cod fillets, 1 lb (500 g)
each, skin intact, pin
bones removed

Coarse salt and freshly
ground pepper

1 tomato, sliced ¼ inch
(6 mm) thick through
stem end

1 yellow summer squash
or zucchini (courgette),
sliced ¼ inch (6 mm) thick
on a sharp diagonal

1 small yellow onion,
sliced

2 tablespoons chopped
fresh basil, cilantro (fresh
coriander), or flat-leaf
(Italian) parsley

Cook the whole potatoes, peels on, in a saucepan of boiling water until tender, about 20 minutes. Drain and let cool. Peel and cut into slices ¼ inch (6 mm) thick.

Preheat the oven to 400°F (200°C). Brush an attractive baking dish in which the fillets will fit in a single layer with ½ tablespoon of the oil. Lay the fillets, skin side down, in the prepared dish. Sprinkle with salt and pepper. Place the potato slices in 2 overlapping rows on top of the cod. Place the tomato slices down the middle, alternating them with the squash slices. Scatter the onion over the top and drizzle with the remaining 1½ tablespoons oil. Sprinkle to taste with salt and pepper.

Bake until the fish is opaque throughout, about 35 minutes. Remove from the oven, sprinkle with the chopped herbs, and serve at once, directly from the dish.

Make-Ahead Tip: The baked cod can be assembled, covered, and refrigerated 1 day in advance of serving. Bring to room temperature and bake as directed.

Variation Tip: Salmon, mahimahi, red snapper, or grouper fillets can be used in place of the cod.

MAKES 6 SERVINGS

SUMMER SQUASHES
Thin-skinned summer squashes come into season in the warm months. The most common varieties are green zucchini (courgettes) and bright-hued yellow squashes, shaped like zucchini or elongated pears. Summer squashes need only be trimmed at the ends before cutting and cooking, for the whole squash—flesh, seeds, and peel—is edible. They can also be stuffed and baked. Look for small or medium-sized summer squashes, as large ones can be watery and bitter.

STRIPED BASS IN GREEN CURRY

In a large sauté pan, heat the canola oil over medium heat. Add the red onion and sauté until softened, about 3 minutes. Stir in the green curry paste, then the coconut milk. Reduce the heat to low and simmer for 5 minutes to blend the flavors.

Add the green beans and cook for 2 minutes. Add the striped bass and simmer gently until opaque throughout, about 5 minutes. Stir in the chopped cilantro.

Transfer to a warmed serving platter or individual plates, garnish with cilantro sprigs, and serve immediately, with hot rice.

Note: Striped bass, sometimes called rockfish around the Chesapeake Bay area, is from the Atlantic. A lean, mild fish, it is well suited to this Thai-inspired curry sauce, which gives it sweetness and piquancy.

Variation Tip: You can also use fillets of cod, halibut, lingcod, salmon, or Chilean sea bass, or chunks of shark or swordfish in place of the striped bass.

MAKES 4 SERVINGS

CURRY PASTE

For homemade curry paste, in a blender, combine 4 jalapeños, seeded and minced; 3 cloves garlic, minced; 2-inch (5-cm) knob fresh ginger, peeled and grated; 1 tablespoon cumin seeds, coarsely ground; 1 table-spoon coriander seeds, coarsely ground; 2-inch (5-cm) piece fresh lemongrass (white part only), peeled and minced, or the grated zest of 1 large lime; 2 tablespoons fresh lime juice; ½ teaspoon dried shrimp paste or 1 teaspoon Asian fish sauce; coarse salt and finely ground black pepper to taste; and ½ cup (4 fl oz/125 ml) water. Purée, then cook in a saucepan over low heat for 5 minutes.

1 tablespoon canola oil

1 red onion, coarsely chopped

1 tablespoon green curry paste, prepared or home-made *(far left)*

1 can (14 fl oz/430 ml) regular or reduced-fat coconut milk

½ lb (250 g) green beans, trimmed and cut into 1½-inch (4-cm) lengths

1½ lb (750 g) striped bass fillet, skin and pin bones removed, cut into 2-inch (5-cm) cubes

3 tablespoons chopped fresh cilantro (fresh coriander), plus sprigs for garnish

1½ cups (10½ oz/330 g) jasmine rice, cooked according to package directions

RED SNAPPER SALAD WITH AIOLI

Coarse salt

1 tablespoon white-wine vinegar

4 red snapper fillets, 6–8 oz (185–250 g) each, skin and pin bones removed

FOR THE AIOLI:

4 cloves garlic, chopped

Coarse salt

2 egg yolks

¼ cup (2 fl oz/60 ml) olive oil

1 cup (8 fl oz/250 ml) canola oil

1 tablespoon fresh lemon juice

½ teaspoon saffron threads steeped in 2 tablespoons dry white wine or water for 15 minutes

Leaves from 1 head butter (Boston) lettuce or Bibb lettuce

2 raw beets, 12 oz (375 g), peeled and coarsely shredded

1 tablespoon capers

Freshly ground pepper

Pour 6 cups (48 fl oz/1.5 l) water into a large sauté pan and add 2 tablespoons salt and the vinegar. Add the red snapper fillets and bring to a boil over medium heat. Reduce the heat to a bare simmer and poach, uncovered, until the fish is opaque throughout, about 5 minutes. Scoop out the fish and set aside to cool.

Meanwhile, make the aioli. In a mortar or bowl, combine the garlic and 1 teaspoon salt and work them together with a pestle or the back of a spoon until they form a coarse paste. Whisk in the egg yolks until blended. Combine the olive and canola oils in a pitcher and whisk into the yolk mixture a drop at a time until the mixture begins to emulsify, or blend. Continue whisking in the oil, now adding it in a thin drizzle. (If the mixture separates, put another egg yolk in a clean bowl. Very gradually whisk in the broken aioli to emulsify it.) Whisk in the lemon juice and the saffron and its steeping liquid. Taste and adjust the seasoning.

Arrange the lettuce leaves on individual plates or a platter. Arrange the fillets on the lettuce and top with spoonfuls of the aioli. Garnish with the beets and capers and sprinkle with pepper. Serve immediately.

Note: This recipe uses raw egg; for more information, see page 113.

Preparation Tip: You can also make the aioli with an electric mixer or in a blender. For the latter, place the garlic, salt, 1 large whole egg, and 1 egg yolk in the blender, then, with the machine running, add the oils in a slow, thin stream. Continue as directed above.

Variation Tip: You can also use fillets of rockfish, skate, orange roughy, pompano, sole, or cod.

MAKES 4 SERVINGS

MAKING AN EMULSION

Aioli is a garlic mayonnaise popular in the south of France. The trick to making aioli, or any mayonnaise, is making a stable emulsion, or blend of two ingredients that do not normally combine—here, oil and lemon juice. Egg yolk is an emulsifier, an agent that helps marry such opposing elements. The oil is very gradually whisked into the egg yolk, one drop at a time, until you see the mixture begin to thicken (above). You may pour the remaining oil in a thin drizzle, still whisking briskly. Once the oil is thoroughly whisked and separated into tiny droplets, the lemon juice may be stirred in.

ROAST SEA BASS WITH
SHIITAKE MUSHROOMS AND BABY CORN

Preheat the oven to 400°F (200°C). Sprinkle the sea bass fillets with the paprika and salt and pepper to taste. Pour the olive oil and wine into an attractive baking dish large enough to hold the fish fillets in a single layer. Scatter the garlic over the bottom of the dish and place the fillets in it. Arrange the mushrooms on top.

Roast for 15 minutes. Baste the mushrooms and fish with the pan juices. Scatter the baby corn ears over the fish and continue to cook, basting once or twice, until the corn is heated through and the sea bass is opaque throughout, about 5 minutes longer. Remove from the oven and garnish with the green onions. Serve immediately, directly from the dish.

Variation Tip: You can use monkfish or salmon fillets or swordfish or shark steaks in place of the sea bass.

MAKES 4 SERVINGS

SHIITAKE MUSHROOMS

Originally from Japan, shiitakes are now grown elsewhere and are readily available. They have light brown caps 2–3 inches (5–7.5 cm) in diameter with pale, creamy-colored gills on their undersides. Pick out mushrooms that look moist. Rather than rinsing, gently brush the mushrooms with a soft brush or damp cloth. Remove and discard the stems. For this recipe, you can substitute 1 oz (30 g) dried shiitakes. Soak them in warm water for 20 minutes to soften, then drain and pat dry with paper towels.

1¾ lb (875 g) sea bass fillets, skinned

2 teaspoons hot paprika or chili powder

Coarse salt and freshly ground pepper

2 tablespoons olive oil

2 tablespoons dry white wine or water

3 cloves garlic, minced

¾ lb (375 g) shiitake mushrooms, brushed clean, stemmed, and sliced

1 can (7 oz/220 g) baby ears of corn, drained and halved on the diagonal

4 green (spring) onions, including tender green parts, thinly sliced on the diagonal

SPECIAL OCCASIONS

The festive dishes in this chapter are perfect for dinner parties. They are not difficult, but they are full of wonderful flavors to surprise and please your guests. It is worth seeking out the more unusual fish and ingredients for a memorable meal.

TUNA TARTARE WITH ANCHOVY AND OLIVE CROSTINI

In a medium bowl, combine the tuna, the ¼ cup olive oil, and the ground peppercorns to taste, mixing well. If desired, cover and refrigerate for at least 30 minutes or up to 3 hours to chill.

To make the olive spread, toast the pine nuts in a small frying pan over medium heat, stirring constantly, until golden, about 4 minutes. Pour onto a plate to cool. In a blender or food processor, combine the toasted pine nuts, olives, red onion, garlic, and oil and process until almost smooth. Set aside.

Preheat the broiler (grill). Arrange the bread slices on a baking sheet and toast, turning once, until crisp, about 5 minutes total. Remove from the broiler, let cool, and cut into 16 strips, each 1 inch (2.5 cm) wide.

Cut the anchovy fillets in half lengthwise. Brush one side of 8 strips of toast with the reserved anchovy oil and top with 2 anchovy slices, placing them in a crisscross fashion. Brush the remaining toast strips with the 2 tablespoons extra-virgin olive oil and spread with the olive spread.

In a small bowl, mix together the chopped fennel, lemon juice, and 1 teaspoon salt.

Just before serving, add the fennel mixture to the chilled seasoned tuna, mixing well. Taste and adjust the seasoning. Garnish with the fennel fronds. Serve with the toasts.

Preparation Tip: Mix the lemon juice and tuna together at the last moment, as the lemon juice will turn the tuna a pinkish gray after about 30 minutes.

MAKES 4 SERVINGS

CHOOSING TUNA

When serving tuna raw, it's important to buy the best available. Visit a high-quality fish market, if possible a Japanese one that supplies sushi restaurants. Ask for sashimi-quality tuna, explaining that you will be serving the fish uncooked. The species will probably be yellowfin tuna, but if you are lucky you may be able to find bluefin. Ask for a small thin sliver to be sure the flesh has no off color, odor, or flavor, and plan to prepare the fish on the same day you buy it.

1¼ lb (625 g) sushi-grade tuna fillet, finely chopped

¼ cup (2 fl oz/60 ml) plus 2 tablespoons extra-virgin olive oil

Mixed green, white, pink, and black peppercorns, ground

FOR THE OLIVE SPREAD:

1 tablespoon pine nuts

¾ cup (4 oz/125 g) brine-cured green olives, pitted

2 tablespoons chopped red onion

2 cloves garlic, chopped

1 tablespoon olive oil

4 slices coarse country bread, each about 4 inches (10 cm) square and ⅓ inch (9 mm) thick, crusts removed

8 olive oil–packed anchovy fillets, drained, oil reserved

½ cup (2½ oz/75 g) finely chopped fennel bulb (page 82), plus fennel fronds for garnish

¼ cup (2 fl oz/60 ml) fresh lemon juice

Coarse salt

ROLLS OF SOLE WITH SPINACH AND SCALLOPS

FOR THE VINAIGRETTE:

2 tomatoes, peeled and seeded (page 86), then chopped

2 tablespoons minced fresh tarragon or flat-leaf (Italian) parsley

1 tablespoon minced shallot

6 tablespoons (3 fl oz/80 ml) olive oil or canola oil

2 tablespoons cider vinegar or fresh lemon juice

Coarse salt and freshly ground pepper

4 sole fillets, 6 oz (185 g) each, skinned

Coarse salt and freshly ground pepper

20 young spinach leaves, stemmed and halved lengthwise

12 medium to large sea scallops, small muscles removed

2 cups (16 fl oz/500 ml) fish stock (page 110) or bottled clam juice

Fresh tarragon or flat-leaf (Italian) parsley sprigs for garnish

To make the vinaigrette, in a blender or food processor, combine the tomatoes, tarragon, shallot, oil, vinegar, and salt and pepper to taste. Blend to make a smooth sauce.

Preheat the oven to 400°F (200°C). Cut each fillet lengthwise into thirds. Place the strips on a work surface, skin side up, and sprinkle with salt. Cover the strips with the spinach leaves. Place a scallop near the slender end of each strip and, starting from that end, roll up the fillet, enclosing the spinach leaves and scallop. Secure with a toothpick. Place the rolls in a baking dish. Pour the stock over the fish.

Bake, basting occasionally, until the scallops are firm and opaque throughout, about 20 minutes.

Just before serving, pour the vinaigrette into a saucepan and warm it over low heat. Pour the vinaigrette onto a warmed platter. Carefully place the fish rolls on the platter, discarding the toothpicks. Sprinkle with pepper, garnish with tarragon, and serve immediately.

Variation Tip: Fillets of flounder, fluke, or sand dab may be substituted for the sole in this recipe.

MAKES 4 SERVINGS

SPINACH PREPARATION

Whether you buy delicate young spinach leaves or large older spinach leaves, it is a good idea to remove the stems, which can be tough and stringy. For larger leaves, fold each leaf in half lengthwise, vein side out. Strip off the stem starting from the thick end. For smaller leaves, simply break off the stems. Wash the spinach carefully. Immerse it in a bowl or sink of cold water, letting the sand sink to the bottom. Lift out the spinach, wash the sand out of the bowl or sink, and repeat until no sand remains.

FRESHWATER FISH IN RED WINE

In a small bowl, work together 1 tablespoon of the butter and the flour with a fork to form a paste, or roux. Set aside. In a saucepan over medium heat, melt the remaining butter. Add the yellow onion, carrot, celery, and ham and sauté until the vegetables begin to soften and turn golden, about 10 minutes.

Tie the parsley and thyme sprigs and the bay leaf in a square of cheesecloth (muslin) to make a bouquet garni. Add to the saucepan. Pour in the wine, bring to a simmer, and cook uncovered until reduced by one-fourth, 20–25 minutes.

Meanwhile, in a large sauté pan over medium heat, fry the bacon pieces, stirring as needed, until crisp, about 5 minutes. Using a slotted spoon, transfer to paper towels to drain. Pour off all but 2 tablespoons of the fat from the pan.

Raise the heat to medium-high, add the onions to the pan, and cook, turning, until browned, about 5 minutes. Using a slotted spoon, transfer to a bowl and set aside. Now add the mushrooms to the pan and sauté until they have released most of their moisture, about 5 minutes. Transfer to the bowl with the onions.

Add the garlic to the pan and sauté over medium heat until tender, about 30 seconds. Place a fine-mesh sieve over the pan and pour the wine mixture through, pressing on the solids with the back of a spoon. Bring to a simmer and whisk in as much of the roux as needed to thicken the wine to a creamy consistency. Cook for 2 minutes, stirring often. Season with salt and pepper.

Lower the heat to medium and add the bacon, onions, mushrooms, and fish. Cook until the fish is opaque throughout, 7 minutes.

Ladle into soup plates, being careful not to break up the fish. Sprinkle with the thyme and serve.

MAKES 4–6 SERVINGS

PEARL ONIONS

Tiny pearl onions, about 1 inch (2.5 cm) in diameter, are white with silvery skins. When cooked, their sweet taste enhances many dishes. To peel them, trim away the root end. Cook in a saucepan of simmering water for 4 minutes. Drain, plunge into cold water to stop the cooking, and drain again. Slip off the skins.

3 tablespoons butter, at room temperature

2 tablespoons flour

½ cup (2½ oz/75 g) *each* chopped yellow onion, carrot, and celery

½ cup (3 oz/90 g) chopped ham

6 fresh parsley sprigs

4 fresh thyme sprigs

1 bay leaf

3½ cups (28 fl oz/875 ml) dry red wine

3 oz (90 g) thick-sliced bacon, coarsely chopped

12 pearl onions, peeled *(far left)*

6 oz (185 g) white button mushrooms, brushed clean

3 cloves garlic, minced

Coarse salt and pepper

1 lb (500 g) assorted freshwater fish such as skinned catfish and carp fillets, cut into 1½-inch (4-cm) pieces

1 trout, head and tail removed, cut into thick crosswise slices

1 tablespoon fresh thyme leaves

SKATE WITH BROWN BUTTER SAUCE

2 lb (1 kg) skinned skate *(far right),* **cut into 4 pieces**

Coarse salt and freshly ground pepper

½ cup (4 oz/125 g) unsalted butter

¼ cup (2 fl oz/60 ml) fresh lemon juice

¼ cup (2 oz/60 g) capers

1 lemon, sliced

Make sure the skate has been skinned. If not, follow the instructions at right. Sprinkle the skate with salt and pepper to taste.

Heat a large sauté pan over medium-high heat, then add half of the butter. When the butter foam subsides, add the skate, reduce the heat to medium, and cook until opaque halfway through, about 4 minutes. Turn the pieces with a wide metal spatula and cook on the second side until the flesh starts to fall off the cartilage, about 3 minutes. Transfer the skate to a warmed serving platter.

Wipe the sauté pan clean with paper towels. Melt the remaining butter over medium heat until it turns brown. Add the lemon juice and capers, swirl the sauce, and pour it over the skate. Serve immediately, with slices of lemon.

MAKES 4 SERVINGS

SKATE

The "wings" of a skate, a member of the ray family, are the part we eat. Thin strands of sweet white meat lie on both sides of thin cartilage. It is best to prepare skate a day or two *after* it has been caught, as its slightly unpleasant odor goes away after it has "rested." Try to find the wings skinned *(above);* if not available, cook them in a large skillet of boiling water with 3 tablespoons distilled white vinegar until the skin starts to come away from the flesh, about 2 minutes. Remove from the water and peel off and discard the skin.

POMPANO BAKED IN SALT

BAKING IN SALT

Baking in salt is a popular cooking method for fish in Portugal and Spain. Cooking whole fish in a salt crust ensures that the flavor and juices are retained—and that the presentation will be dramatic. A whole red snapper, rockfish, fluke, flounder, or sole can be used in place of the pompano.

Preheat the oven to 400°F (200°C). In a large bowl, whisk the egg whites until frothy. Gradually add the fine and coarse salts and the flour and stir until well mixed.

Put the parsley sprigs inside the fish. Brush the outside of the fish lightly with 1 tablespoon of the oil. Cut a piece of cheesecloth (muslin) 20 inches (50 cm) long and 15 inches (38 cm) wide. Wrap the fish in the cheesecloth and set aside.

Spread a third of the salt mixture in a baking pan large enough to hold the fish. Lay the fish on top and cover with the remaining salt mixture. Bake until the salt has turned pale brown and an instant-read thermometer inserted into the thickest part of the fish behind the head registers 140°F (60°C), about 40 minutes.

Meanwhile, in a saucepan, heat the remaining 2 tablespoons olive oil over medium heat. Add the bell peppers, onion, garlic, and carrot, stirring well. Reduce the heat to low, cover, and cook, stirring occasionally, until the vegetables are soft, about 25 minutes. Remove from the heat and transfer to a blender or food processor. Add the lemon juice and vinegar and process to form a smooth sauce. Add a splash of warm water if the mixture seems too thick. Season with salt and white pepper to taste. Set aside and keep warm.

The next step may be done at the table for a dramatic presentation. Using a large spoon or a hammer, break up the salt crust, then spoon it into a large bowl. Be careful not to pierce the fish. When the fish is fully exposed, remove the cheesecloth, brushing it with warm water if needed. Peel the skin from the fish and place the whole fish on a warmed platter, or lift the fillets off the backbone and place on a warmed platter. Pour the sauce over and around the fish and sprinkle with the diced bell pepper. Serve at once.

MAKES 4 SERVINGS

4 egg whites

4 cups (2 lb/1 kg) fine salt

4 cups (2 lb/1 kg) kosher salt

1 cup (5 oz/155 g) all-purpose (plain) flour

6 fresh flat-leaf (Italian) parsley sprigs

1 whole pompano, about 2 lb (1 kg), skin intact, cleaned by the fishmonger

3 tablespoons olive oil

2 yellow bell peppers (capsicums), seeded and chopped

1 small yellow onion, chopped

2 cloves garlic, minced

¾ cup (3½ oz/105 g) coarsely grated carrot

1 tablespoon fresh lemon juice

1 tablespoon cider vinegar

Coarse salt and freshly ground white pepper

Finely diced green bell pepper (capsicum) or black sesame seeds for garnish

GINGERY MONKFISH WITH CRISPY NOODLES

½ cup (1½ oz/45 g) sesame seeds

½ cup (2½ oz/75 g) peeled and grated fresh ginger

1 cup (8 oz/250 g) granulated sugar

Coarse salt

½ teaspoon cayenne pepper

2 lb (1 kg) monkfish fillet, skin and dark membrane removed by the fishmonger, cut crosswise on the diagonal into 4 pieces

1 cup (8 fl oz/250 ml) rice vinegar

½ cup (4 fl oz/125 ml) fresh lime juice

¼ cup (2 fl oz/60 ml) fish sauce

¼ cup (2 oz/60 g) tomato paste

½ cup (3½ oz/105 g) firmly packed dark brown sugar

3 tablespoons grated lemon zest

Canola oil

2 oz (60 g) dried rice flour noodles (rice vermicelli)

Fresh cilantro (fresh coriander) sprigs for garnish

Spread the sesame seeds on a plate. In a small bowl, stir together the ginger, half of the granulated sugar, 4 teaspoons salt, and the cayenne. Coat the fish pieces evenly with the ginger mixture, then roll them in the sesame seeds, pressing lightly so the seeds adhere well. Set aside. In a small saucepan, whisk together the vinegar, lime juice, fish sauce, tomato paste, the remaining granulated sugar, the brown sugar, lemon zest, and ½ teaspoon salt. Set aside.

Pour oil to a depth of 4 inches (10 cm) in a Dutch oven or deep-fryer and heat until it registers 350°F (180°C) on a deep-frying thermometer. Put the noodles in a paper or plastic bag and break them up a little. Working in 4 batches, lower the noodles into the hot oil with a wire-mesh skimmer and fry, turning as necessary, until they puff up and turn opaque, about 30 seconds. Scoop out the noodles and transfer to paper towels to drain. Cover loosely with aluminum foil to keep warm.

In a large sauté pan, heat 2 tablespoons oil over medium heat. Add the fish and sauté, turning once, until browned on both sides, about 3 minutes total. Watch carefully, as the sugar in the rub will color the fish quickly. Reduce the heat and cook the fish until opaque throughout, about 4 minutes. Meanwhile, place the pan holding the vinegar mixture over low heat and warm to serving temperature, stirring occasionally.

Transfer the monkfish to warmed individual plates and arrange the noodles around it. Drizzle the warm sauce over the fish and noodles. Garnish with cilantro sprigs. Serve immediately.

Note: Use caution when deep-frying. For tips, see page 21.

MAKES 4 SERVINGS

DRIED RICE FLOUR NOODLES

Available in Asian groceries and well-stocked super-markets, these long, skinny noodles, also called rice sticks or rice vermicelli, can be soaked to soften them or deep-fried to crisp them, as in this recipe. Before cooking, break them up in a bag so that they can be deep-fried in batches and so that the cooked noodles will be easier to eat.

ESCABECHE OF TROUT

In a saucepan, combine the vinegar, wine, saffron, carrot, bay leaves, and dried chile. Bring to a boil over medium-high heat, reduce the heat to medium-low, and simmer for 30 minutes to blend the flavors.

Meanwhile, in a sauté pan, heat 2 tablespoons of the oil over medium-high heat. Add the yellow onion and garlic and sauté until they start to color, about 5 minutes. Reduce the heat to medium-low and stir in the sugar. Cook, stirring occasionally, until golden, about 15 minutes longer.

Add the yellow onion mixture to the vinegar mixture and simmer for 10 minutes. Remove from the heat, season to taste with salt and pepper, and set aside.

In a shallow bowl, stir the flour and paprika together and season well with salt and pepper. Taste for flavor. Dredge the fish in the seasoned flour, coating evenly and shaking off the excess.

In a large sauté pan, heat the remaining 3 tablespoons oil over medium-high heat. Add the fish, in batches if necessary, and cook, turning once, until golden brown on both sides but still translucent in the center, about 6 minutes total. Transfer the fish to a deep serving dish. Place a lemon slice on each fish.

Return the vinegar mixture to a boil, add the green onions, and cook until wilted, about 1 minute. Pour over the fish and let stand until the fish is cooked through, about 10 minutes. Serve hot or at room temperature.

Variation Tip: You can use other small whole fish, such as sardines, bluefish, rockfish, or snapper, or steaks or fillets of cod, mahimahi, redfish, or orange roughy.

MAKES 6 SERVINGS

2½ cups (20 fl oz/625 ml) distilled white or cider vinegar

2 cups (16 fl oz/500 ml) dry red wine

1 teaspoon saffron threads

1 carrot, peeled and coarsely grated

4 bay leaves

1 small dried red chile, seeded

5 tablespoons (3 fl oz/80 ml) canola or olive oil

1 yellow onion, sliced

4 cloves garlic, sliced lengthwise

1 tablespoon sugar

Coarse salt and freshly ground pepper

1 cup (5 oz/155 g) all-purpose (plain) flour

1 tablespoon hot paprika

6 cleaned and boned whole trout, about 8 oz (250 g) each

6 lemon slices

4 green (spring) onions, including tender green parts, halved lengthwise and cut into 2-inch (5-cm) lengths

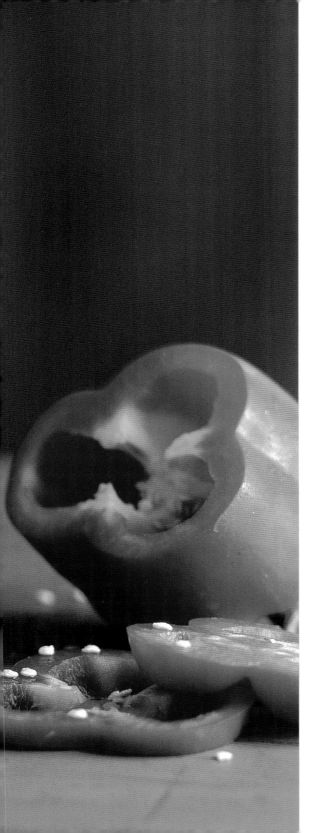

ON THE GRILL

Grilling can be one of the easiest and most delicious ways to cook almost all types of fish. Cooking over an open fire adds terrific flavor, and there's no better way to enjoy warm weather than alfresco dining. But when the weather turns cold and damp, a grill pan on the stove top is a good approximation of the real thing. For helpful tips on grilling, turn to page 109.

HALIBUT STEAKS WITH
CITRUS, WATERCRESS, AND BLACK OLIVES

MARINATING TIPS

Marinating is a way of adding flavor to and, in some cases, tenderizing food. A marinade commonly includes flavorful additions such as ginger, garlic, and herbs or spices. It usually contains some acid as well, such as lemon juice, wine (used here), or vinegar. Tough cuts of meat are sometimes soaked in a marinade for hours to improve their texture. Fish, however, is naturally tender and should not be marinated for more than 20 minutes in an acidic marinade. Otherwise, the fish will "cook" in the acid.

Prepare a fire in a charcoal grill or preheat a gas grill. Meanwhile, combine the wine, molasses, and ginger in a bowl and whisk together. Pour into a shallow casserole or baking dish. Lay the halibut steaks in the marinade, turn to coat, and let stand at room temperature for 20 minutes (but no longer).

Drain the halibut, letting the marinade drip back into the dish; pat dry, brush with the oil, and sprinkle to taste with salt and pepper. Reserve the marinade. Grill the steaks over direct heat until browned on the first side, 3–5 minutes, depending on thickness. Using a wide metal spatula, turn the fish and cook until browned on the second side and opaque throughout, 3–4 minutes.

Meanwhile, place the orange and lemon wedges directly on the grill and cook, turning once, until lightly browned on each side, about 2 minutes total. Transfer the fish and orange and lemon wedges to individual plates or a platter. In a small saucepan, boil the reserved marinade for 2 minutes. Pour over the halibut and garnish with the watercress and black olives.

Note: The molasses included in the marinade helps the fish brown without overcooking it. You won't taste the sweetness.

Variation Tips: Other fish steaks, such as striped bass, swordfish, tuna, shark, and mahimahi, can be used instead of halibut. To cook on the stove top, use a preheated grill pan over high heat.

MAKES 4 SERVINGS

¾ cup (6 fl oz/180 ml) dry white wine

2 tablespoons light molasses

2 tablespoons peeled and finely grated fresh ginger

4 halibut steaks, 6–8 oz (185–250 g) each

2 tablespoons canola oil

Coarse salt and freshly ground pepper

1 orange, cut into 8 wedges

1 lemon, cut into 4 wedges

1 bunch watercress, stemmed

½ cup (2½ oz/75 g) Kalamata olives

SALMON WITH FENNEL AND APPLE SALSA

FOR THE SALSA:

1 fennel bulb, trimmed (page 82) and finely chopped, fronds reserved for garnish

1 Granny Smith apple, unpeeled, cored, and diced

3 tablespoons fresh lemon juice

Coarse salt and freshly ground pepper

4 salmon fillets, 6–8 oz (185–250 g) each, or 1½ lb (750 g) salmon fillet in one piece, skin and pin bones removed

½ cup (4 fl oz/125 ml) fresh lemon juice

2 teaspoons sugar

¼ cup (2 oz/60 g) barbecue sauce (far right)

2 tablespoons fennel seeds plus extra for garnish

To make the salsa, combine the fennel, apple, 3 tablespoons lemon juice, and salt and pepper to taste in a bowl. Cover the salsa and set aside.

Prepare a fire in a charcoal grill or preheat a gas grill. Score the skin side (see Note, page 10) of each salmon fillet with 2 shallow crisscross cuts. In a large nonaluminum bowl, stir together the ½ cup lemon juice, sugar, and barbecue sauce. Add the salmon, turn to coat, and let stand for 10 minutes (but no longer).

Just before cooking the salmon, throw the 2 tablespoons fennel seeds on the coals, or add the seeds in a perforated aluminum foil packet to a gas grill (see Note). Lift the salmon from the marinade, letting the marinade drip back into the bowl, and reserve the marinade. Lay the salmon on the grill over direct heat and cook until browned on the first side, about 5 minutes. Using a wide metal spatula, turn and cook on the second side until opaque throughout, about 3 minutes longer.

Spoon the salsa onto individual plates or a serving platter. Lay the fish on the salsa. In a small saucepan, boil the reserved marinade for 2 minutes. Pour over the salmon, garnish with fennel seeds, and serve.

Note: To make a perforated foil packet for the fennel seeds, place the seeds on a sheet of heavy-duty aluminum foil and fold the up the edges to completely enclose the seeds. Perforate the top of the packet with a fork or the tip of a knife.

Variation Tips: Dill or fennel fronds can be thrown on the coals to add more flavor to the smoke. Striped bass, bluefish, shad, mackerel, or arctic char fillets can be used instead of the salmon. To cook on the stove top, use a preheated grill pan over high heat. Just before adding the salmon, sprinkle the pan with 1 teaspoon fennel seeds.

MAKES 4 SERVINGS

BARBECUE SAUCE

To make barbecue sauce, in a small saucepan over medium-high heat, combine ½ yellow onion, finely chopped; 2 minced cloves garlic; 1 cup (8 oz/250 g) ketchup; ⅓ cup (3 fl oz/80 ml) red wine vinegar; ¼ cup (2 oz/ 60 g) packed brown sugar; 1 tablespoon Dijon mustard; 1 tablespoon Worcestershire sauce; and 1 teaspoon hot-pepper sauce. Bring to a boil, stirring constantly. Reduce the heat to low and simmer, uncovered, until the sauce is thick and the flavors blended, about 15 minutes. Remove from the heat and let cool before using. Makes about 2 cups (16 oz/500 g).

STRIPED BASS WITH LEEKS AND BALSAMIC VINAIGRETTE

To make the vinaigrette, in a small bowl, whisk together the vinegar and mustard. Gradually whisk in the oil in a fine stream to make an emulsified, or blended, sauce. Add salt and pepper to taste. Set aside.

In a mortar, mash the garlic and 2 tablespoons salt together with a pestle or the back of a spoon. Rub the fish with the garlic and sprinkle with pepper to taste. Set aside.

Prepare a fire in a charcoal grill or preheat a gas grill. In a large saucepan of salted boiling water, cook the leeks until nearly tender, about 10 minutes. Drain and set aside. Brush the fish and leeks lightly with the olive oil.

Place the fish and leeks on the grill (or, for thin fillets, place in a grill basket) over direct heat and cook until browned on one side, 2–3 minutes. Turn and cook on the second side until the fish and leeks are browned on the outside and the fish is opaque throughout, 2–3 minutes longer. To serve, drizzle the vinaigrette onto individual plates and place the fish and leeks on top.

Variation Tips: Red snapper, grouper, salmon, rockfish, or cod can be used instead of striped bass. To cook on the stove top, use a preheated grill pan over high heat.

MAKES 4 SERVINGS

FOR THE VINAIGRETTE:

¼ cup (2 fl oz/60 ml) balsamic vinegar

½ cup (4 oz/125 g) Dijon mustard

¾ cup (6 fl oz/180 ml) olive oil

Coarse salt and freshly ground pepper

8 cloves garlic, minced

Coarse salt and freshly ground pepper

1½ lb (750 g) striped bass fillets or 4 striped bass steaks, each 6–8 oz (185–250 g) and 1 inch (2.5 cm) thick

4 leeks, white and tender green parts only

2 tablespoons olive oil

BALSAMIC VINEGAR

A slightly sweet taste and a luscious dark caramel color characterize balsamic vinegar. It is a fermentation made from the "must," or first crush, of white Trebbiano grapes. *Tradizionale* balsamic vinegars are carefully barreled and aged, sometimes for decades; this type of vinegar is used in small quantities as a prized condiment. A young *tradizionale* balsamic or a high-quality supermarket balsamic is more appropriate for this recipe.

MONKFISH KABOBS WITH MIXED VEGETABLES

2 tablespoons light
molasses

1 cup (8 fl oz/250 ml) dry
white wine

1½ lb (750 g) monkfish
fillet, skin and dark
membrane removed by
the fishmonger

8 cherry or miniature pear
tomatoes

1 red bell pepper
(capsicum), seeded and
cut into 1-inch (2.5-cm)
squares

1 small red onion, cut into
1-inch (2.5-cm) chunks

2 large portobello mush-
rooms, brushed clean,
stemmed, and sliced
½ inch (12 mm) thick

¼ cup (2 fl oz/60 ml) plus
2 tablespoons extra-virgin
olive oil

Coarse salt and freshly
ground pepper

4–8 thick slices coarse
country bread

1 clove garlic, halved

1 lemon, quartered

4 long wooden skewers,
soaked in water for
20 minutes, or metal
skewers

Prepare a fire in a charcoal grill or preheat a gas grill. In a bowl, mix together the molasses and wine. Cut the monkfish into 1½-inch (4-cm) cubes and add to the bowl. Turn to coat the fish. Let stand at room temperature for 20 minutes.

Drain the monkfish. To make the kabobs, alternately thread the cherry tomatoes and the bell pepper, the onion, and the mushroom pieces with 4 pieces of the fish on each skewer. Brush the kabobs with the 2 tablespoons olive oil and season to taste with salt and pepper.

Place the kabobs on the grill over direct heat and cook, turning them to brown on all sides, until the fish is opaque throughout, about 5 minutes. At the same time, toast the slices of bread on the grill, rub them with halved pieces of garlic, and brush with the ¼ cup olive oil. Serve, garnished with the lemon quarters.

Note: The molasses included in the marinade helps the fish brown without overcooking it. You won't taste the sweetness.

Variation Tips: Other firm-fleshed fish, such as salmon, mahimahi, shark, swordfish, or halibut, also make good kabobs. Or, use shellfish such as shrimp or scallops. To cook on the stove top, use a preheated grill pan over high heat.

MAKES 4 SERVINGS

WOODEN SKEWERS

If using wooden skewers,
soak them in water for at
least 20 minutes so they
won't burn on the grill.
To help prevent scorching
the skewer, push the food
together on the skewer and
wrap the end in aluminum
foil to make a handle.
If you grill often and like
to make kabobs, look for a
set of metal skewers for
convenience.

TUNA BURGERS

Prepare a fire in a charcoal grill or preheat a gas grill. In a bowl, combine the chopped tuna, onion and its juice, the 2 tablespoons mayonnaise, and salt and pepper to taste. Shape into 4 firm patties about 3 inches (7.5 cm) in diameter and 1½ inches (4 cm) thick. Cover and chill in the freezer for no longer than 10 minutes.

Meanwhile, to make the lemon-chive mayonnaise, stir together the ¼ cup mayonnaise, salt and pepper to taste, lemon juice, 1 tablespoon chives, soy sauce, and hot-pepper sauce in a small bowl. Set aside.

Carefully place the tuna patties on the grill with a wide spatula. Grill the patties, gently turning once, until lightly browned, about 5 minutes total for medium-rare, 8 minutes total for medium. At the same time, lightly toast the bread slices on the grill. Transfer to individual plates.

Place the tuna patties on half of the bread slices. Top with the lettuce leaves, tomato slices, and the 1 tablespoon snipped chives. Garnish with wedges of dill pickle. Serve immediately, with the lemon-chive mayonnaise on the side.

Note: This recipe uses raw egg; for more information, see page 113.

Variation Tips: If you like, mix 1 lb (500 g) tuna with ½ lb (250 g) white fish, such as halibut or sole. To cook on the stove top, use a lightly oiled preheated grill pan over high heat.

MAKES 4 SERVINGS

FRESH MAYONNAISE
Homemade mayonnaise tastes much better than jarred: In a bowl, combine 1 large egg yolk, 1 teaspoon Dijon mustard, and a pinch of coarse salt. Whisk together. Very gradually whisk in ¾ cup (6 fl oz/180 ml) olive oil, a drop at a time until the mixture begins to thicken. Continue whisking and pouring in the remaining oil in a thin stream. Season with freshly ground white pepper. Add 1 teaspoon lemon juice or more to taste. Store in a covered jar in the refrigerator for up to 10 days. Makes ¾ cup (6 fl oz/180 ml).

1½ lb (750 g) tuna fillet, finely chopped

2 tablespoons coarsely grated yellow onion and its juice

2 tablespoons mayonnaise

Coarse salt and freshly ground pepper

FOR THE LEMON-CHIVE MAYONNAISE:

¼ cup (2 fl oz/60 ml) fresh or prepared mayonnaise

Coarse salt and freshly ground pepper

2 tablespoons fresh lemon juice

1 tablespoon snipped fresh chives

1 teaspoon soy sauce

½ teaspoon hot-pepper sauce

8 slices brioche or challah, each 1 inch (2.5 cm) thick, or 4 kaiser rolls, split

4 crisp lettuce leaves

1 tomato, sliced

1 tablespoon snipped fresh chives

2 dill pickles, cut into lengthwise wedges

SARDINE FILLETS IN GRAPE LEAVES

8 fresh or bottled grape leaves

8 sardines, heads removed, cleaned, and boned by the fishmonger if possible (see Note)

1 bunch fresh mint, stemmed and finely chopped

2 tablespoons grated lemon zest

Coarse salt and freshly ground pepper

2 tablespoons hot-pepper sauce

3 tablespoons olive oil

1 lemon, quartered

Prepare a fire in a charcoal grill or preheat a gas grill. Meanwhile, blanch the grape leaves in a saucepan of boiling water for 1 minute. Scoop them out with a skimmer or slotted spoon, rinse in cold water, and pat dry.

Spread the sardines open, skin side down, on a work surface. In a small bowl, combine the mint, lemon zest, and salt and pepper to taste. Stir to blend. Divide the mint mixture evenly among the sardines, spreading it over the flesh. Close the sardines and brush the outsides with the hot-pepper sauce. Place the leaves, veined side up, on a work surface. Lay a sardine near the stem end of a grape leaf and fold the leaf over the fish. Fold in the sides and roll the sardine up inside the leaf. Repeat with the remaining leaves and sardines. Brush the packets with the olive oil.

Place the sardine packets on the grill over direct heat and cook, turning once, until the sardines are opaque throughout, about 8 minutes total. Don't worry if the leaves char; this will add flavor. Toward the end of cooking, place the lemon quarters directly on the grill and cook, turning once, until browned on both sides, about 3 minutes total.

Transfer the sardine packets to warmed individual plates or a platter and garnish with the lemon quarters. Serve immediately.

Note: To bone a headless cleaned sardine, with your fingers, loosen the backbone near the tail end and pull it out, working toward the head. Spread the sardine open. You will see tiny rib bones, which can be left, but any larger bones should be removed.

Variation Tip: Boned red mullet, anchovies, smelt, or whiting can also be prepared this way. Leaf-wrapped sardines or other fish can also be cooked under a preheated broiler (grill) or on a stove-top grill pan preheated over high heat.

MAKES 4 SERVINGS

GRAPE LEAVES

Grape leaves are available in jars, preserved in a water and vinegar brine, or in some areas they can be found fresh on the vine. Both preserved and fresh leaves should be blanched—briefly boiled, then rinsed with cold water to halt the cooking. In the case of the former, this rids them of some of their vinegary taste; in the case of the latter, it tenderizes them. Whichever leaves you use, make sure they are large enough to enclose the sardines.

MAHIMAHI WITH TOMATILLO DIP

Prepare a fire in a charcoal grill or preheat a gas grill. Meanwhile, make the tomatillo dip. In a small, dry frying pan over medium-high heat, toast the pumpkin seeds until they pop and brown slightly, about 5 minutes. Pour onto a plate and set aside.

In the same pan, heat 2 tablespoons of the canola oil over medium heat. Add the onion and garlic and sauté until soft, about 5 minutes. Reduce the heat to medium-low and add the tomatillos, chile, and cumin. Stir well, cover, and cook, stirring once or twice, until the tomatillos are soft, about 5 minutes.

Transfer the tomatillo mixture to a blender or food processor and add the pumpkin seeds, stock, cilantro, and parsley. Process until smooth. Season to taste with salt and pepper. Divide among individual dipping bowls.

In a large nonaluminum bowl, whisk the lime juice, hot-pepper sauce, molasses, and remaining 1 tablespoon oil together. Cut the fish fillets into horizontal slices ¾ inch (2 cm) thick and then into 2-by-4-inch (5-by-10-cm) pieces. Add the fish pieces to the marinade, turn to coat, and let stand for 5 minutes. Thread the fish onto the skewers, dividing the fish evenly among them.

Place the skewers on the grill over direct heat and cook, turning once, until browned on the outside and opaque throughout, about 5 minutes total.

Transfer the skewers to a warmed platter or individual plates. Serve with the dipping sauce alongside.

Variation Tip: Shrimp (prawns) or thinly sliced shark or swordfish can be used in place of the mahimahi. To cook on the stove top, use a preheated grill pan over high heat.

MAKES 4 SERVINGS

TOMATILLOS

Resembling small green tomatoes, tomatillos are 1–2 inches (2.5–5 cm) in diameter and covered with a papery husk, which must be removed before cooking. Tomatillos are found in Latin markets and are acidic rather than sweet. To prepare them, use your fingers to peel off the papery husks under warm running water. The husks and the sticky, resinous substance that coats the fruits beneath the husks will rinse right off. Tomatillos are usually chopped and cooked before they are added to a sauce or salsa.

FOR THE TOMATILLO DIP:

¾ cup (3 oz/90 g) hulled pumpkin seeds

3 tablespoons canola oil

1 small white onion, chopped

3 cloves garlic, minced

½ lb (250 g) tomatillos, husked *(far left)* and quartered

1 jalapeño chile, seeded and minced

½ teaspoon ground cumin

1 cup (8 fl oz/250 ml) chicken stock or broth

2 tablespoons chopped fresh cilantro (coriander)

2 tablespoons chopped flat-leaf (Italian) parsley

Coarse salt and pepper

¼ cup (2 fl oz/60 ml) fresh lime juice

2 tablespoons hot-pepper sauce

1 tablespoon molasses

1½ lb (750 g) mahimahi fillets

4 wooden skewers, soaked in water for 20 minutes, or metal skewers

HEARTY DISHES

Fish is an excellent choice for a light, quick supper, but that's not the only role fish can play. Some types can also be slowly braised or stirred into a risotto for a hearty, satisfying dish. The recipes that follow are warming, often one-pot meals that are well worth the extra time they require. Needing minimal accompaniment, they can be doubled to provide a meal for a second night.

SEAFOOD SAUSAGES WITH MUSTARD SAUCE
AND POBLANO MASHED POTATOES

ROASTING CHILES AND PEPPERS

To peel chiles and peppers and give them a nice texture, roast them. Preheat the broiler (grill). Cut the chile or bell pepper in half lengthwise and remove the stem and seeds. Place the halves, cut side down, on a baking sheet and broil them 5 inches (13 cm) from the heat source until the skin blackens and blisters, about 6 minutes. Remove from the broiler, cover loosely with aluminum foil, and let steam and cool for 10 minutes. Peel away the black skin.

To make the mustard sauce, blanch the spinach in a pot of salted boiling water for 30 seconds. Drain, rinse under cold running water, and squeeze dry. In a blender or food processor, combine the spinach, canola oil, mustard, vinegar, parsley, tarragon, and 1 teaspoon salt. Process until smooth. Transfer the mixture to a small saucepan and keep warm over low heat.

Meanwhile, cook the potatoes, whole and skin on, in a saucepan of salted boiling water until tender when pierced with a knife, 20–40 minutes, depending on size. Add the garlic cloves during the last minute of cooking. Drain the potatoes and garlic and set the garlic aside. Rinse the potatoes under cold water until cool to the touch, then peel them.

In a small saucepan, combine the milk and butter and heat over low heat until the butter melts. Add the cayenne and salt and black or white pepper to taste. Remove from the heat.

Push the potatoes and garlic through the fine disk of a food mill or a ricer placed over a warmed bowl. (Alternatively, mash with a fork or potato masher.) Add the warmed milk mixture and the poblano chile and beat with a wooden spoon until smooth. Taste and adjust the seasoning. Cover and set aside.

Heat a large frying pan or grill pan over medium heat, then brush with olive oil. Prick each sausage a few times with a fork and add to the pan. Fry, turning to brown the sausages on all sides, until opaque throughout, about 10 minutes. Serve the sausages and mashed potatoes on warmed plates along with the mustard sauce.

Note: Seafood sausages, usually made of salmon, shrimp, scallops, herbs, and egg whites, can be found in the supermarket seafood case.

MAKES 4 SERVINGS

FOR THE MUSTARD SAUCE:

½ lb (250 g) spinach, stemmed

6 tablespoons (3 fl oz/80 ml) canola oil

¼ cup (2 oz/60 g) Dijon mustard

2 tablespoons cider vinegar

½ cup (½ oz/15 g) chopped fresh flat-leaf (Italian) parsley

2 tablespoons chopped fresh tarragon

Coarse salt

1¾ lb (875 g) Yukon gold or russet potatoes, unpeeled

8 cloves garlic

¾ cup (6 fl oz/180 ml) milk

¼ cup (2 oz/60 g) unsalted butter

⅛ teaspoon cayenne pepper

Coarse salt and ground white or black pepper

1 poblano chile, roasted and peeled *(far left)*, then minced

1 tablespoon olive oil

1½ lb (750 g) seafood sausages (see Note)

SWORDFISH STEAKS PROVENÇALE

4 swordfish steaks, each
6–8 oz (185–250 g) and
1 inch (2.5 cm) thick,
skinned

4 oil-packed anchovy
fillets, drained, each cut
into 3 equal pieces

2 tablespoons extra-virgin
olive oil

1 cup (5 oz/155 g) finely
chopped yellow onion

3 cloves garlic, minced

2 cups (24 oz/750 g)
peeled, seeded, and
chopped tomatoes
(page 86), or 1 can
(28 oz/875 g) chopped
plum (Roma) tomatoes,
with some juice

2 tablespoons tomato
paste

¾ cup (6 fl oz/180 ml) dry
white wine

2 tablespoons balsamic
vinegar or red-wine
vinegar

Coarse salt and freshly
ground pepper

15 fresh basil leaves,
shredded

12 black olives such as
Niçoise or Kalamata

1 tablespoon grated
lemon zest

Make 3 small incisions in each swordfish steak and insert a piece
of anchovy into each incision; they may protrude a bit.

In a large sauté pan, heat 1 tablespoon of the olive oil over medium
heat. Add the onion and garlic and sauté until golden, about
5 minutes. Add the tomatoes, tomato paste, wine, vinegar, and
salt and pepper to taste. Cook, stirring frequently, until thickened,
about 10 minutes. Remove from the heat and keep warm.

In another large sauté pan, heat the remaining 1 tablespoon oil over
medium-high heat. Add the swordfish steaks and cook, turning
once, until lightly browned on both sides, about 5 minutes total.
Spoon the tomato sauce over the fish and cook for 1 minute.

Using a slotted spatula, transfer the fish to warmed individual
plates or a platter. Stir the basil, olives, and lemon zest into the
tomato sauce, heat it briefly, and pour it over the swordfish. Serve
immediately.

*Variation Tip: You can substitute steaks such as tuna, shark, halibut,
or salmon for the swordfish. The same sauce also complements
chicken or pasta.*

Serving Tip: Serve with steamed young fennel or green beans.

MAKES 4 SERVINGS

BLACK OLIVES
Cured black olives are
made in many different
Mediterranean countries,
including Greece, France,
Italy, and Spain. For this
Provençal dish, try Niçoise
olives from the south of
France; they are small and
not too pungent. Other not-
too-salty olives are Greek
Kalamatas. These delicious
black olives are fairly large
with pointed ends. Both
kinds are traditionally used
unpitted. Canned or bottled
black ripe olives are not
suitable for this dish.

BAKED ORANGE ROUGHY WITH ZUCCHINI AND TOMATO

Preheat the oven to 425°F (220°C). In a bowl, coat the zucchini with 1 tablespoon of the olive oil.

Lay the fish fillets on a plate in a single layer. Arrange the zucchini slices on the fillets, overlapping them to resemble scales. Press down to secure in place and sprinkle with salt and pepper to taste. Cover and refrigerate.

In a medium sauté pan, heat 2 tablespoons of the oil over medium-high heat. Add the shallots and sauté until translucent, about 2 minutes. Add the garlic and sauté until soft, about 1 minute. Add the tomatoes and sugar and season with salt and pepper to taste. Bring to a boil, reduce the heat to medium-low, and simmer uncovered for 5 minutes to blend the flavors. Stir in the dill.

Pour the tomato sauce into an attractive baking dish large enough to accommodate the fish fillets in a single layer. Place the fish on top of the tomato sauce. Bake until the fish is opaque throughout, about 20 minutes. Remove from the oven, garnish with the lemon quarters, and serve directly from the baking dish.

Make-Ahead Tip: This dish can be fully assembled up to 3 hours in advance, covered, and refrigerated.

Variation Tip: Sole, tilefish, rockfish, red snapper, bluefish, grouper, or shad fillets can stand in for the orange roughy.

MAKES 4 SERVINGS

2 zucchini (courgettes), about 1 lb (500 g) total weight, cut into slices ⅛ inch (3 mm) thick

4 tablespoons (2 fl oz/ 60 ml) olive oil

4 orange roughy fillets, 6–8 oz (185–250 g) each, with skin intact

Coarse salt and freshly ground pepper

3 shallots, minced

2 cloves garlic, minced

1 can (28 oz/875 g) crushed tomatoes

1 teaspoon sugar

¼ cup (⅓ oz/10 g) chopped fresh dill

1 lemon, quartered

MAKING THIN SLICES
The zucchini slices used in this recipe should be paper thin, almost translucent. This may be achieved with a chef's knife and some patience, but a mandoline makes thin slicing a snap. The food is moved over the very sharp blades of the tool with a strumming motion, which gives the mandoline its name. Metal French mandolines and plastic Asian slicers are both available. If your model does not have a hand guard, keep your hand as flat as possible and your fingers away from the blades when slicing.

RISOTTO WITH CHILEAN SEA BASS AND LEEKS

5 cups (40 fl oz/1.25 l) fish stock (page 110) or bottled clam juice

2 tablespoons olive oil

1 lb (500 g) leeks, white part only, quartered lengthwise and chopped

4 green (spring) onions, including some tender green parts, sliced

3 cloves garlic, minced

1½ cups (10½ oz/330 g) Arborio rice or other medium-grain rice

1 cup (8 fl oz/250 ml) dry white wine

1¼ lb (625 g) Chilean white sea bass fillets, skin and pin bones removed, cut into 1½-inch (4-cm) cubes

3 tablespoons minced fresh rosemary, plus sprigs for garnish

Coarse salt and freshly ground white pepper

2 tablespoons grated lemon zest

In a saucepan, bring the stock to a boil over medium-high heat. Reduce the heat to low and maintain at a low simmer.

In a large, heavy saucepan, heat the olive oil over medium heat. Add the leeks, green onions, and garlic and sauté until wilted, about 3 minutes. Add the rice and stir until opaque, about 2 minutes.

Add the wine and cook, stirring, until nearly evaporated. Add a ladleful of the simmering stock, reduce the heat to low, and cook, stirring, until the stock is nearly absorbed, about 3 minutes. Continue adding stock in this manner, keeping the grains slightly moist at all times and stirring continuously, until the rice is nearly al dente (tender yet still firm at the center of each kernel), about 25 minutes total.

Add the fish, minced rosemary, and salt and white pepper to taste. Cook, stirring gently so as not to break up the fish, for about 3 minutes. Taste the rice and continue to cook until the rice is al dente and the fish is opaque throughout, about 3 minutes longer.

Stir in the grated lemon zest. Transfer to warmed individual soup plates or a serving dish. Garnish with rosemary sprigs and serve immediately.

Serving Tip: Follow this all-white dish with a brightly colored salad, such as tomato and red bell pepper (capsicum).

Variation Tip: Rockfish, red snapper, black sea bass, whitefish, or weakfish can be used in place of the Chilean sea bass.

MAKES 4 SERVINGS

RISOTTO SAVVY

Risotto is made from specific varieties of rice classified as medium-grain in the United States and short-grain in Europe. The most common is Arborio. The rice is naturally coated with a layer of starch that gives risotto its wonderful creamy texture. Baldo, Vialone Nano, and Carnaroli are other varieties of medium-grain rice with a starchy layer. The key to good risotto is to add hot stock to the rice little by little, letting the rice slowly absorb the liquid before you add more stock. Do not let the risotto come to a full boil, but cook at a gentle simmer so that the rice has time to slowly swell and soften.

ROCKFISH BRAISED WITH FENNEL AND ONIONS

Preheat the oven to 400°F (200°C). In a large sauté pan, heat the oil over medium-high heat. Add the onion, celery, carrot, fennel, and garlic and sauté until soft, about 5 minutes. Stir in the chopped dill and salt and pepper to taste. Transfer two-thirds of the vegetable mixture to an ovenproof baking dish large enough to hold the fish flat.

Lay the fish on top of the vegetables, then scatter the remaining vegetables on top. Place the same sauté pan over medium heat and add the white wine. Bring to a simmer and deglaze the pan, stirring to scrape up any browned bits from the pan bottom. Simmer for 1 minute and pour over the fish and vegetables. Cover the dish with aluminum foil.

Bake, basting occasionally with the pan juices, until the fish is opaque throughout and an instant-read thermometer inserted into the thickest part of the fish behind the head registers 140°F (60°C), about 30 minutes.

Remove from the oven and carefully transfer to a warmed platter. Garnish with dill sprigs and serve at once.

Variation Tip: This dish can also be prepared with whole red snapper, striped bass, or bluefish.

MAKES 4 SERVINGS

FENNEL PREPARATION

This pale green bulb with slender stalks and fronded leaves imparts a subtle anise flavor. To prepare fennel for cooking, first trim the bulb of any browned bits. Cut off the long stalks from the bulb and use only the bulb, trimming away the base of the core if it is thick and tough. Halve the bulb crosswise and lay the halves cut side down for stability. Cut the bulb halves into thin lengthwise slices.

3 tablespoons canola oil or olive oil

1 cup (3½ oz/105 g) sliced yellow onion

1 cup (4 oz/125 g) sliced celery

1 cup (5 oz/155 g) peeled, halved, and sliced carrot

1 cup (4 oz/125 g) sliced fennel

2 cloves garlic, minced

2 tablespoons chopped fresh dill, plus sprigs for garnish

Coarse salt and freshly ground pepper

1 whole rockfish, 2 lb (1 kg), cleaned by the fishmonger

1 cup (8 fl oz/250 ml) dry white wine

PAELLA

2 tablespoons olive oil

2 thick slices bacon, diced

1 large onion, chopped

4 cloves garlic, minced

1 green bell pepper (capsicum), seeded and chopped

2 cups (14 oz/440 g) rice for paella (see Note)

1 teaspoon dried oregano

1 teaspoon ground coriander

4 cups (32 fl oz/1 l) bottled clam juice or water

2 Spanish chorizo sausages, sliced ¼ inch (6 mm) thick

4 canned whole tomatoes, chopped

1 teaspoon saffron threads

¾ lb (375 g) shrimp (prawns)

¾ lb (375 g) cleaned squid

¾ lb (375 g) monkfish, cod, or bass fillets, skin and pin bones removed

1½ lb (750 g) mussels, scrubbed and debearded if necessary (page 97)

¾ cup (6 fl oz/180 ml) dry white wine

Coarse salt and pepper

1 cup thawed frozen baby peas

In a heavy flameproof casserole dish or Dutch oven, heat the oil over medium-high heat. Add the bacon and cook until crisp, about 2 minutes. Reduce the heat to medium. Add the onion and cook until soft, about 4 minutes; add the garlic and bell pepper and cook until soft, about 5 minutes longer. Stir in the rice, oregano, and coriander. Stir until the rice is opaque, about 2 minutes. Heat the clam juice and add it with the chorizo, tomatoes, and saffron. Mix well, cover, and cook over low heat until most of the liquid is absorbed and the rice is almost tender, about 25 minutes. Stir occasionally as the rice cooks and add a splash of water if it becomes dry.

As the rice is cooking, prepare the seafood. Peel and devein the shrimp (page 93). Cut the squid into ¼-inch (6-mm) rings (page 98). Cut the fish fillets into 1-inch (2.5-cm) cubes. Set aside.

Meanwhile, put the mussels and wine in a covered pot, discarding any that do not close to the touch. Steam the mussels until the shells open, about 5 minutes. Discard any that do not open. Remove the mussels and set aside. Strain the broth through cheesecloth (muslin) or a fine sieve placed over a bowl. Add salt and pepper to taste. Add the shrimp, squid, fish, peas, and mussel broth to the paella and cook for 5 minutes.

To serve, garnish the paella with the mussels.

Note: Bomba, Calasparra, and Arborio rice are good for making paella. In a pinch, substitute long-grain rice and increase the cooking time by 5–10 minutes before adding the shellfish.

Serving Tip: If desired, garnish the paella with thin strips of serrano ham, capers, or thin strips of roasted and peeled red bell peppers (capsicums).

MAKES 6–8 SERVINGS

COOKING PAELLA

Although somewhat lengthy in its preparation, Spanish paella is a grand dish to serve at a celebratory event. It is best to prepare the ingredients well in advance and start cooking the paella an hour before serving time. A wide, shallow paella pan is authentic but more difficult to cook in, as it does not come with a cover and on the stove top the food may cook unevenly. Some find a small burnt area of rice delicious, but for other cooks, using a flameproof casserole or Dutch oven is a more carefree and reliable method.

BRAISED MONKFISH WITH
BACON AND TOMATOES

In a heavy flameproof casserole dish or Dutch oven, heat the oil over medium-high heat. Add the bacon and garlic and sauté until the bacon is fairly crisp and the garlic is beginning to brown, about 5 minutes. Push the bacon and garlic to the side and lay the monkfish in the dish. Sear until lightly browned on both sides, using tongs to turn the fish. Sprinkle lightly with salt and pepper. Add the tomatoes and pile most of them and the bacon mixture on top of the monkfish.

Add the white wine and basil and stir to scrape up any browned bits from the bottom. Reduce the heat to low, cover, and cook for about 20 minutes, or until the flesh starts to pull away from the backbone.

Serve the fish on a warmed platter, surrounded and topped with the vegetables.

Note: Monkfish has firm white flesh attached to a central bone, and there are no rib bones with which to contend. Cooked in one piece, monkfish absorbs flavors well; bacon, tomatoes, garlic, and basil suit it perfectly.

Variation Tip: Thick mahimahi or sand shark fillets can be used instead of the monkfish.

MAKES 4 SERVINGS

PEELING TOMATOES

To peel tomatoes, bring a pot of water to a boil. Using a sharp knife, cut a shallow X in the bottom end of each tomato. Have ready a bowl of ice water. Immerse the tomatoes in the boiling water and blanch them for 15 seconds, then, using a slotted spoon, transfer them to the ice water to stop the cooking. Peel the tomatoes with your fingers or a small knife. To seed, slice the tomatoes in half crosswise and lightly squeeze and shake, using your finger if needed to help dislodge the seeds.

2 tablespoons olive oil

6 thick slices bacon, cut into 1-inch (2.5-cm) pieces

1 head garlic, cloves separated and peeled

3–4 lb (1.5–2 kg) monkfish on the bone, skin and dark membrane removed by the fishmonger

Coarse salt and freshly ground pepper

4 tomatoes, peeled and seeded *(far left),* then coarsely chopped

1 cup (8 fl oz/250 ml) dry white wine

1 tablespoon chopped fresh basil

SHELLFISH

The bounty of shellfish we enjoy from coasts around the world seems almost limitless, including bivalves such as clams, oysters, mussels, and scallops as well as crustaceans such as crabs, lobsters, and shrimp. Some shellfish must be bought live, and most are cooked only briefly to bring out the best of their fresh, clean flavors and delicate textures.

CRAB CAKES WITH ROUILLE

Preheat the oven to 450°F (230°C). Line a standard 12-cup muffin pan with 10 paper liners. Fill the remaining 2 empty cups halfway with water (this will prevent the pan from warping in the hot oven). If using fresh corn kernels, cook them in a small saucepan of salted boiling water until tender, about 3 minutes. Drain and set aside.

In a sauté pan over medium heat, fry the bacon until crisp, about 5 minutes. Using a slotted spoon, transfer the bacon to paper towels to drain.

In a bowl, stir the mayonnaise, mustard, egg, black pepper to taste, and cayenne together. Add the corn, bacon, crabmeat, chives, tarragon, and ½ cup (2½ oz/75 g) of the cornmeal. Divide into 10 equal portions and form each portion into a cake that will fit snugly into a lined muffin cup. Spread the remaining cornmeal on a plate and coat the cakes evenly. Insert each cake into a lined muffin cup.

Bake until golden, about 15 minutes. Remove from the muffin-cup liners, transfer to a warmed platter, and serve with the rouille and toast triangles.

Note: French for "rust," rouille is a traditional accompaniment to many fish dishes, especially bouillabaisse (page 17). A spicy sauce usually containing peppers (capsicums) or chiles, garlic, and olive oil, rouille has a thick consistency and can be blended into fish stock, spread on toasted baguette slices, or served as a garnish, as seen here.

Variation Tip: Flaked cooked fish, such as salmon, tuna, cod, sole, or red snapper, or chopped cooked shrimp can be used in place of the crabmeat.

MAKES 5 SERVINGS

ROUILLE

To make rouille, cook 1 peeled, quartered russet potato in a saucepan of boiling water until tender, 15 minutes. Drain and coarsely chop. In a small frying pan, heat ¼ cup (2 fl oz/60 ml) olive oil over medium heat. Add 4 halved cloves garlic and sauté until golden, about 1 minute. Transfer the garlic and oil to a blender or food processor. Add 2 coarsely chopped roasted red bell peppers (page 74), the potato, 1 teaspoon saffron dissolved in 1 tablespoon dry white wine, ¼ cup (2 fl oz/ 60 ml) water, 1 tablespoon fresh lemon juice, and 2 pinches of cayenne. Process until smooth. Season with salt and pepper.

1 cup (6 oz/185 g) fresh or thawed frozen corn kernels

4 slices bacon or pancetta, finely chopped

3 tablespoons mayonnaise

2 tablespoons Dijon mustard

1 egg, beaten

Freshly ground black pepper

2 pinches of cayenne pepper

1½ lb (750 g) fresh lump crabmeat, picked over for shell fragments

3 tablespoons snipped fresh chives

2 tablespoons chopped fresh tarragon

¾ cup (4 oz/125 g) coarse cornmeal

Rouille for serving *(far left)*

5 slices white bread, crusts removed, toasted and cut into triangles

SPAGHETTI WITH CLAMS

SERVES 4

Coarse salt
1 pound spaghetti
2 tablespoons olive oil
2 cloves garlic, minced
1 small dried chile pepper, crumbled, or pinch of red-pepper flakes
1½ pounds littleneck clams, scrubbed
1 cup dry white wine
2 tablespoons coarsely chopped fresh flat-leaf parsley,
plus whole leaves for garnish
Juice of 1 lemon
3 tablespoons unsalted butter
Freshly ground black pepper

1. Bring a large pot of water to a boil; salt generously. Add spaghetti, and cook until slightly underdone, about 7 minutes. Drain pasta, reserving 1 cup of cooking liquid. Set aside.
2. Meanwhile, heat oil in a large skillet over medium heat. Add garlic and chile pepper; cook until garlic is golden, about 2 minutes. Add clams and white wine, and raise heat to high. Bring to a boil; cover, and cook, shaking occasionally, 2 to 3 minutes, until clams open. Stir in parsley. Transfer to a bowl; set aside.
3. Return skillet to medium-high heat. Add reserved pasta water and lemon juice; reduce until slightly thickened, about 2 minutes. Remove from heat; whisk in butter. Add clam mixture and spaghetti. Cook over medium-low heat until heated through, 2 to 3 minutes. Season with salt and pepper; garnish with parsley.

SHRIMP SAUTÉED WITH LEMON AND GARLIC

4 tablespoons (2 fl oz/ 60 ml) olive oil

1¼ lb (625 g) large shrimp (prawns), peeled and deveined, tail intact

6 cloves garlic, minced

Coarse salt and freshly ground pepper

2 green (spring) onions, including tender green parts, thinly sliced

2 tablespoons chopped fresh flat-leaf (Italian) parsley

¼ cup (2 fl oz/60 ml) fresh lemon juice

In a large sauté pan, heat 2 tablespoons of the oil over medium-high heat. Add half of the shrimp to the pan and cook until pink on one side, about 1 minute. Turn the shrimp over with tongs, add half of the garlic, and cook until pink on the second side, just a few seconds. Add salt and pepper to taste, toss, and quickly add half of the green onions, parsley, and lemon juice. Toss again and transfer to a warmed platter. Wipe the pan clean with paper towels and repeat with the remaining shrimp and other ingredients. Serve immediately.

Note: Shrimp need only a small handful of seasonings and brief cooking to bring out their naturally sweet flavor.

Variation Tip: Sea or bay scallops can be prepared in the same way.

MAKES 4 SERVINGS

DEVEINING SHRIMP

If the vein that runs along the back of shrimp is clearly apparent, it is often removed for reasons of looks and texture. Usually, only large or jumbo shrimp need deveining. Peel the shrimp, leaving the tail segment intact, if you like. Use a small knife to cut along the curved back of the shrimp and remove the exposed vein. For recipes calling for unpeeled shrimp, cut down along the back through the shell with kitchen scissors and leave the shell in place when you remove the vein.

SEA SCALLOPS WITH PANCETTA

Preheat the oven to 450°F (230°C). Lay the pancetta slices on a work surface and sprinkle evenly with the thyme. Place a scallop on its rounded side in the center of each pancetta slice and wrap the pancetta snugly around the scallop, overlapping the ends of the pancetta. Brush a baking dish with the olive oil and pour ½ cup (4 fl oz/125 ml) of the water into the dish. Place the wrapped scallops upright in the baking dish, arranging them side by side.

Pour water to a depth of 1½ inches (4 cm) into a saucepan. Put the egg yolks in a heatproof bowl large enough to fit on top of the saucepan without touching the water and whisk to blend. Add the wine and the remaining ½ cup water and whisk to combine. Set aside. Bring the water in the saucepan to a boil. Reduce the heat to a simmer.

Put the scallops in the oven and bake until the pancetta is crisp and the scallops are opaque throughout, about 8 minutes.

Meanwhile, place the bowl with the yolk mixture over (but not touching) the simmering water. Whisk until the mixture forms a very thick and foamy sauce, about 8 minutes. Season to taste with salt and pepper and remove from the heat.

Whisk the snipped chives into the sauce. Transfer the scallops to warmed individual plates or a platter. Pour the sauce around the scallops. Garnish with the whole chives. Serve at once.

Variation Tip: Peeled shrimp (prawns) or the meat from lobster tails can be used in place of the scallops.

MAKES 4 SERVINGS

PREPARING SCALLOPS
Scallops found still in their shells are a rare treat, and it is more likely that you'll find them already shelled at the market. The adductor muscle is the part of the scallop that we eat. It joins the shells of this bivalve together. With large sea scallops, about 14 per pound (500 g), the tough white tissue on the side of each scallop is very apparent. Just pull it off and discard. Look for day-boat, or diver, scallops which are fresher than those kept in a preservative solution.

20 paper-thin slices pancetta about 1 inch (2.5 cm) wide

2 tablespoons minced fresh thyme, or 1 tablespoon dried thyme

1½ lb (750 g) large sea scallops, small muscles removed

1 tablespoon olive oil

1 cup (8 fl oz/250 ml) water

4 egg yolks

½ cup (4 fl oz/125 ml) dry white wine

Coarse salt and freshly ground pepper

2 tablespoons snipped fresh chives, plus 8 whole chives for garnish

MUSSELS WITH TOMATOES AND FENNEL

2 tablespoons olive oil

½ fennel bulb, trimmed and finely chopped, fennel fronds reserved for optional garnish

4 cloves garlic, sliced lengthwise

4 large tomatoes, peeled and seeded (page 86), then chopped

1 tablespoon tomato paste

1 cup (8 fl oz/250 ml) dry white wine

4 lb (2 kg) mussels, scrubbed and debearded if necessary *(far right)*

1 tablespoon grated orange zest

Leaves from 2 large fresh basil sprigs, coarsely chopped, plus small whole leaves for optional garnish

Coarse salt and freshly ground pepper

1 tablespoon Pernod or other anise-flavored liqueur

Preheat the oven to 400°F (200°C). In a large sauté pan, heat the olive oil over medium heat. Add the chopped fennel and garlic and sauté until they begin to color, about 5 minutes. Add the tomatoes and tomato paste, stir well, and simmer uncovered for 10 minutes. Remove from the heat and keep warm.

In a large saucepan over medium heat, bring the wine to a boil. Reduce the heat to low and cook for 3 minutes. Raise the heat to medium and add the mussels, discarding any that do not close to the touch. Cover and cook, shaking the pan periodically, until all the mussels are fully opened, about 5 minutes. Discard any that failed to open. Stir once. Remove from the heat and let cool.

Pull off and discard one shell from each mussel and lay the mussels, still in their single shells, on a rimmed baking sheet. Strain the cooking juices through cheesecloth (muslin) or a fine sieve over a bowl and save for another use, or reserve to serve hot in mugs or soup bowls with the sauced mussels.

Return the tomato-fennel sauce to medium heat. Add the orange zest, chopped basil, and salt and pepper to taste and stir in the Pernod.

Meanwhile, place the baking sheet with the mussels in the oven and bake until the mussels are heated through, about 1 minute.

Pour a little of the sauce onto warmed plates. Divide the mussels evenly among the plates. Place teaspoonfuls of the remaining sauce on the mussels at the rounded end of each shell. Garnish with basil leaves and/or a few fennel fronds. Serve immediately.

Serving Tip: Accompany the mussels with a salad of mixed greens and wedges of country bread. The sauce is also delicious with pasta.

MAKES 4 SERVINGS

MUSSEL VARIETIES

For this dish, you can use small blue mussels; larger, more tender Mediterranean mussels; or green-lipped mussels from New Zealand and China. Blue mussels are found in both the Atlantic and Pacific oceans, but most that we buy nowadays are farmed. This is to our advantage because they arrive at the market very clean and often beardless, so that all you have to do is immerse them in a sinkful of cold water and rub them together. If the mussels do have beards—the strings that attached them to their rock— just pull them off right before cooking. Green-lipped mussels are available fresh or frozen.

LINGUINE WITH RED SHELLFISH SAUCE

In a large saucepan, heat the olive oil over medium-high heat. Add the onion and sauté until golden, about 5 minutes. Add the garlic and sauté until golden, about 30 seconds. Add the tomatoes, wine, and tomato paste, reduce the heat to medium, and cook uncovered until slightly thickened, about 10 minutes. Season to taste with salt and pepper, stir in the lemon zest, and remove from the heat and keep warm.

In a large pot of salted boiling water, cook the linguine until it is al dente, 8–10 minutes.

While the pasta is cooking, put the clams in a large saucepan, discarding any that do not close to the touch. Add ¼ cup (2 fl oz/ 60 ml) water, cover the pan, and cook the clams over medium heat, shaking the pan periodically, for 3 minutes. Add the mussels, again discarding any that do not close to the touch, and cook until the mussels and clams open, 2–3 minutes longer. Discard any shellfish that failed to open. Strain the pan juices through cheese-cloth (muslin) or a fine-mesh sieve over a bowl and set aside.

Meanwhile, return the tomato sauce to medium heat. Add the shrimp and cook for 1 minute. Add the squid rings and cook until the shrimp are pink and the squid are opaque, about 1 minute longer. Add the clams and mussels and their reserved juices. Stir in 1 tablespoon of the parsley.

Drain the linguine and put it in a warmed bowl. Spoon the sauce over the pasta, garnish with the cherry tomatoes, and sprinkle with the remaining 1 tablespoon parsley. Serve immediately.

Variation Tip: This easy-to-assemble dish of pasta and shellfish can be made with other types of pasta, such as spaghetti, spaghettini, and fettuccine. You can also use a variety of shellfish, as in this recipe, or just one kind.

MAKES 4 SERVINGS

CLEANING SQUID

You can buy squid whole or cleaned. To clean squid yourself: Pull the head and tentacles away from the body, or tube-like part, of the squid. Reach into the tube, pull out the insides, and discard. Make sure you find and discard the plasticlike quill. Rinse the tube out. Cut off the tentacles above the eyes. Squeeze the cut end of the tentacles to remove the hard, round "beak" at the base and discard it. Trim all the tentacles to the same length. Repeat with the remaining squid. If the squid are already cleaned, just rinse them out.

2 tablespoons olive oil

1 small yellow onion, chopped

4 cloves garlic, minced

1 can (28 oz/875 g) plum (Roma) tomatoes, diced, with juice reserved

½ cup (4 fl oz/125 ml) dry red wine

2 tablespoons tomato paste

Coarse salt and pepper

2 teaspoons grated lemon zest

½ lb (250 g) dried linguine

12 littleneck clams or ¾ lb (375 g) Manila clams, scrubbed

1 lb (500 g) mussels, scrubbed and debearded if necessary (page 97)

½ lb (250 g) medium shrimp (prawns), peeled and deveined (page 93)

½ lb (250 g) cleaned squid bodies *(far left)*, cut into ¼-inch (6-mm) rings

2 tablespoons chopped fresh flat-leaf (Italian) parsley

12 cherry tomatoes, cut into quarters

WARM OYSTERS WITH LEEK AND BACON SAUCE

6 slices bacon, coarsely chopped

3 tablespoons unsalted butter

½ lb (250 g) leeks, including tender green parts, finely chopped

1 cup (8 fl oz/250 ml) dry white wine

2 cups (16 fl oz/500 ml) heavy (double) cream

Coarse salt and freshly ground white pepper

24–36 oysters on the half shell, liquor reserved (far right)

3 tablespoons chopped fresh dill or snipped fresh chives

Preheat the oven to 375°F (190°C). In a large sauté pan over medium heat, fry the bacon until crisp, about 5 minutes. Using a slotted spoon or spatula, transfer the bacon to paper towels to drain and cool. Finely crumble. Pour off all but 1 tablespoon of the fat from the pan.

Return the sauté pan to medium heat and add the butter. When the butter foam subsides, add the leeks and sauté until they just begin to soften, about 1 minute. Add the wine and cook until slightly reduced, about 5 minutes.

Reduce the heat to low, add the cream, and bring to a simmer. Cook until the sauce thickens, about 5 minutes. Add the bacon and season to taste with salt and white pepper. Remove from the heat and keep warm.

Spread the shucked oysters on the half shells in a single layer in a baking dish. Bake until the oysters plump up and their edges curl, about 7 minutes. Meanwhile, pour the oyster liquor into the sauce and stir well. Return to low heat.

Transfer the oysters to warmed individual plates. Spoon the sauce over the oysters, garnish with the dill, and serve at once.

Preparation Tip: To save time in the kitchen, ask your fishmonger to shuck the oysters, reserving the shells and oyster liquor. Use the shucked oysters within a few hours.

Serving Tip: It is best to serve oysters in the winter months when the waters are icy cold and shellfish are at their peak.

MAKES 6 SERVINGS

OYSTERS ON THE HALF SHELL

Scrub the oysters with a stiff brush and rinse well. Grip an oyster, flat side up, with a folded kitchen towel. Push the tip of an oyster knife into one side of the hinge, opposite the shell's concentric ridges, and pry upward to open the shell. Keeping the blade edge against the inside of the top shell, run the knife all around the oyster to sever the muscle that holds the shell halves together. Lift off and discard the top shell, catching any spilled oyster liquor in a bowl. Run the knife underneath the oyster to loosen it from the shell.

STEAMED LOBSTER WITH DRAWN BUTTER

In 1 or 2 pots large enough to hold all the lobsters, pour water to a depth of ¾ inch (2 cm) and bring to a boil over high heat. Add 3 tablespoons salt and place a collapsible steamer basket in the pot. Pick up the lobsters by their heads with your hands or tongs and place on the steamer basket. Cover the pot and reduce the heat to medium. Cook for 15 minutes for small lobsters or 25 minutes for larger ones, counting the cooking time from the moment you put them in the pot.

Meanwhile, melt the butter in a small saucepan over low heat. Divide among 4 ramekins or small bowls. Squeeze a few drops of lemon juice from 2 of the lemon halves and add a sprinkle of salt into each container of melted butter.

Using tongs, transfer the lobsters to the kitchen sink and rinse them under cold running water to stop the cooking.

If using small lobsters, serve them whole. If using large lobsters, halve each lobster by cutting through the underside of the shell from head to tail. Alternatively, crack the lobsters and remove their meat *(left)*. Place each whole lobster, half lobster, or one-fourth of the lobster meat on an individual plate accompanied by a ramekin of melted butter. Place a lettuce leaf, a slice or two of tomato, and a lemon half on each plate for garnish. If serving whole or halved lobsters, be sure there are lobster or nut crackers and lobster picks for everyone.

Note: Lobsters should show signs of life either in the fish tank or on ice before you purchase them. Once home, store the lobsters in the refrigerator surrounded by damp newspaper or seaweed in an open bag, so that they can breathe.

MAKES 4 SERVINGS

CRACKING LOBSTER

To make it easy for your guests to eat lobsters, crack them before serving. First pull off the claws and knuckles and detach the tail from the body. Pull off the legs and reserve. Place the claws on a board and, using a hammer or mallet, tap the shells and extract the meat in pieces as large as possible. Discard the shells. Using scissors, cut down the middle of the underside of the tail, spread the shell open, and extract the tail meat in one piece. Slice and arrange on individual plates in a decorative fashion.

Coarse salt

4 small live lobsters, 1¼ lb (625 g) each, or 2 large live lobsters, 2½ lb (1.25 kg) each

2 cups (1 lb/500 g) unsalted butter

3 lemons, halved

4 crisp lettuce leaves

1 tomato, sliced

FISH BASICS

Hundreds of different types of fish, both wild and farmed, are eaten around the world. These denizens of both fresh and salt water cook quickly and are healthful and delicious. Read on to find out how to choose and prepare fish.

ABOUT FISH

Fish are available in an amazing range of sizes and shapes. Think of giant tuna weighing hundreds of pounds, and then of tiny anchovies, which can be eaten in one bite.

Some fish are flat and swim horizontally. Known collectively as flatfish, the most common examples are flounder, fluke, halibut, and sole. Most fish, however, are round bodied and swim vertically.

Nearly all fish are sold already filleted because today's cooks do not want to contend with bones. If you are dealing with a whole fish, you can easily fillet it yourself (page 107), or you can ask the fishmonger to fillet it for you. But cooking a fish whole has its advantages, too: its flesh is especially moist since it is protected from the heat by the skin.

Many fish are lean and, when cooked, have a delicate taste and a soft and flaky texture. Sole, flounder, bass, snapper, skate, cod, perch, and whitefish are good examples. Other fish, including swordfish, halibut, tuna, monkfish, and mahimahi, have firm, springy flesh. Some fish that are oily and have an especially strong taste are mackerel, bluefish, salmon, and sardines. Generally, fish take little time to cook, so you can often count on a quick preparation.

CHOOSING FISH

Buy fish from a specialized market or supermarket fish counter with good turnover. It is best to go to the market with no fixed idea of the fish you want and to purchase what looks freshest and most appealing. Most fish are caught year-round, but some have a season, which factors into availability.

Use all your senses to choose fish. In a market in which the fish is packaged, pick it up and inspect it. If it has an off odor, pass it by. Touch the fish; it should feel firm, not flabby. The eyes of a whole fish should be clear, the scales intact, and the tail moist. Besides whole fish, you can also purchase steaks, cross-sectional cuts containing a small section of the backbone, or fillets, boneless portions cut from the sides of the fish. Both steaks and fillets should have solid flesh with no gaps.

Shellfish should look wholesome and clean. All bivalves, like clams, mussels, and oysters in the shell, must be alive. If they are, their shells will close tightly when you touch them. (The exceptions are cockles and soft-shelled clams, whose shells are always partially open.) Live crabs and lobsters should show signs of life either in their tanks or on ice.

Frozen fish is fine if it has been professionally flash frozen (home freezers are not cold enough to keep fish frozen properly for long). Defrost frozen fish slowly in the refrigerator.

Serve ¼ to ½ pound (125 to 250 g) of fish fillets or steaks per person and about twice that amount when whole.

STORING FISH

Unwrap purchased fish or shellfish, place it on a plate or in a bowl, and then rewrap and refrigerate. Live shellfish, such as oysters, mussels, clams, and lobsters, must be kept alive in the refrigerator, with their wrappings open so they can breathe.

For the best taste, cook and eat the fish or shellfish the day you buy it.

HOW TO CLEAN AND FILLET A FISH

If you are an avid angler—or know one—you may have occasion to clean a whole fish yourself. All it takes is a little practice.

First, remove the fish's fins with scissors if desired. Be careful, as some fins can be quite spiny. (Leave the fins if you plan to cook the fish whole for a more dramatic presentation.)

Next, using a fish scaler or the blunt edge of a knife blade, scale the fish: Holding the fish by the tail, let it hang down into a plastic bag or a sink full of water. (The scales will fly in all directions.) Starting at the tail end and working down to the head, scrape the scales from the fish and rinse it well.

Clean the fish by cutting into the cavity from belly side, the anal vent up to the head. Remove and discard the entrails and rinse the fish well.

Shown opposite are the basic steps for filleting a round fish:

1 **Making the first cut**: Place the cleaned fish on a cutting board at an angle, with the head pointing away on your right (if you are right-handed) and the back facing you. Using a sharp boning knife, make a crosswise cut just below the gill to separate the flesh from the head. Now, starting at the head, run the knife along the back, cutting through the skin, until you reach the tail (opposite, top left). Make a crosswise cut to separate the flesh from the tail.

2 **Retracing to make a deeper cut**: Retrace the cut along the back, cutting in with long, smooth strokes until you feel the backbone with the tip of your knife (opposite, top right).

3 **Cutting the flesh from the rib bones**: Lift up the edge of the flesh, revealing the ribs. Cut the flesh away from the ribs, starting at the back and following the curve of the ribs with the knife (opposite, bottom left). As you cut, keep the knife in contact with the bones to remove as much flesh as possible. Do not remove the fillet from the bones yet, as you will need the bulk to fillet the other side successfully.

4 **Removing the fillet on the second side**: Turn the fish over and make crosswise cuts to separate the flesh from the head and tail. Starting at the tail end, make another cut along the backbone. Proceed as above, cutting the flesh away starting at the backbone, then up over the ribs and down to the belly cavity. Remove the fillet from the bones (opposite, bottom right). Turn the fish over and lift off the first fillet.

After being filleted, fish can be skinned and cut into chunks or cubes (for skewers), medaillons, steaks, or scallops. They can also be split or butterflied.

Flatfish like sole and flounder can be treated in much the same way. Cut all the way around the cavity and proceed as above. The cavity on a flatfish is very small, and the fish does not have protruding rib bones.

SKINNING FILLETS

To skin a fillet, place it skin side down on a cutting board along the edge nearest you, with the tail end on the side of your nondominant hand. Using the nails of your nondominant hand, firmly hold onto the skin on the bottom of the fillet. Insert a chef's knife at an angle between the skin and flesh. Pull and push the knife toward the head, holding the tail end firmly with your other hand while you separate the flesh from the skin using the knife.

REMOVING PIN BONES

A row of small pin bones protrudes slightly through the flesh of all fish fillets from the head end and above where the belly cavity was. Run your fingers over fillets to find the bones and pull them out with special fish tweezers or clean needle-nosed pliers—or, if they are very soft, as in salmon, pull them out with your fingers. Sometimes the bones are so securely fixed into the flesh that it is best to cut them out. Using a paring knife, slit the flesh on either side of the bones; pull out the bones and the small amount of attached flesh, and discard them.

For information on preparing mussels, see page 97; deveining shrimp, page 93; preparing scallops, page 94; opening oysters, page 101; removing lobster meat, page 102; and cleaning squid, page 98.

COOKING FISH AND SHELLFISH

Fish is one of the most versatile foods you can prepare. Its mild flavor and firm texture can be matched with a wide variety of flavors and cooking methods. Most fish and shellfish take a relatively short time to cook, so it is crucial to get it right. (The best fish for different cooking methods follow.)

BEST FISH TO GRILL

Firm-fleshed fillets, steaks, split fish, and whole fish, such as tuna, salmon, shark, halibut, monkfish, striped bass, bluefish, black sea bass, mahimahi, and swordfish, are all good choices for grilling. Mackerel will also do well on the grill. Delicate flounder or sole fillets placed directly on a grill are likely to fall apart. Shellfish such as scallops, shrimp (prawns), squid, and lobster are superb cooked on the grill.

Grill baskets, made from hinged wire grids, can simplify grilling delicate fish fillets or whole fish, which can sometimes stick to the grill rack and fall apart when turned. Use them, too, for grilling small fish and shellfish that otherwise might fall through the rack into the fire. To help prevent sticking, brush the inside surfaces of the basket with oil.

BEST FISH TO BROIL

Fish fillets, such as those from shad, arctic char, whitefish, or red snapper, or fish steaks, such as those from salmon, cod, swordfish, and tuna, may be easily broiled in the oven. Whole fish can be difficult to broil because of their girth. For basic broiling instructions, turn to page 110. Be sure to pour $\frac{1}{8}$ inch (3 mm) of dry white wine or water into the pan before broiling and to place the fish fillets as close as possible to the heat source.

BEST FISH TO BAKE

Any filleted fish may be baked. For baking recipes in this book, turn to page 33 or 78. Use a shallow baking pan and be sure to pour $\frac{1}{8}$ inch (3 mm) of dry white wine or water into the pan before baking. This prevents the fillets from sticking to the pan.

BEST FISH TO OVEN-POACH

Whole fish, such as salmon, bluefish, snapper, and grouper, or fillets of bass, snapper, salmon, or grouper may be oven-poached. See page 18.

BEST FISH TO ROAST

Whole fish of all sizes, such as red snapper, salmon, bluefish, sardines, pompano, and whitefish, may be roasted. For roasting recipes in this book, turn to page 26 or 38.

BEST FISH TO DEEP-FRY (WITH BATTER)

Fillets of cod, sole, fluke, and catfish, as well as shrimp and steamer clams, are good choices for deep-frying. See page 21.

BEST FISH TO SAUTÉ

All fillets, such as those from sole, tilefish, swordfish, and Pacific rock-fish, are good for sautéing. See page 10 or 13.

BEST FISH TO BAKE IN PARCHMENT

Any fillets or steaks, such as those from halibut, trout, baby coho salmon, salmon, red snapper, or bass, may be baked in parchment. See page 30.

BEST FISH FOR USING IN SOUPS, STEWS, AND PASTA SAUCES

Whiting, trout, monkfish, and salmon, as well as mussels, clams, and squid, are all excellent in soups, stews, and pasta sauces. See pages 14, 85, and 98.

JUDGING DONENESS

One of the most important things when cooking fish is to recognize when it has just finished cooking. Fish that is undercooked or over-cooked is not usually palatable.

Following are three ways to use to recognize when fish is cooked to the correct degree of doneness.

1. Touch the fish with your finger. It should be as firm as the tip of your nose. The more experience you have cooking fish, the easier it is to judge doneness by touch.

2. The flesh, which is translucent before cooking, must be opaque all the way through. (The exceptions are tuna and salmon, which are often eaten medium-rare to rare.) Make a small incision in the flesh with a knife in an inconspicuous place to check.

For shrimp, cut off a slice from the head end to see if it is opaque. For lobster, the cooking time is calculated according to weight, since the flesh, trapped in the shell, cannot be checked. Follow the recipe directions for timing. Mussels and clams are ready as soon as they open. When cooking *en papillote* (in a parchment paper package), the timing is calculated according to the thickness of the fillet. Plan on 10 minutes per inch (2.5 cm) at the thickest part, then open a packet to check for doneness.

3. The foolproof method of testing for doneness is to use an instant-read thermometer. Insert the thermometer into the thickest part of the fish away from the backbone, which conducts heat. The fish is cooked when it reaches 140°F (60°C).

GRILLING BASICS

Grilling is one of the simplest and best ways to cook fish. A few guidelines will guarantee the best results.

For charcoal grills, let the coals burn for a few minutes beyond the point at which they are covered with white ash. The fire should be hot, so that the fish will be well seared. Hold your hand over the grill rack and count. If you can count up to only one or two before you need to pull your hand away, the coals are very hot—fine for a beef steak but not for a fish fillet. If you can count up to three or so, you're ready to grill. If using a gas grill, it's only a matter of turning a dial.

For indirect grilling in a charcoal grill, suitable for cooking whole large or small fish and very thick fillets or steaks, stack the coals on one side of the grill and place the food opposite. It is a slower and gentler way to grill. When grilling indirectly, keep the grill lid closed but the vents open; the heat and smoke trapped inside will help to cook the fish and give it a delicious smoky flavor.

For indirect grilling on a gas grill, open the fuel valve of the propane tank, light the flames as directed by the manual, and preheat on high heat. Turn one burner off and keep the other burner on high heat. Place the food over the unlit side and cover the grill.

Bring any fish to room temperature before grilling. Cook large and small whole fish, like sardines, in hinged grill baskets of the appropriate size, so that you can turn the fish without their falling apart.

If possible, use real charcoal rather than briquettes. If desired, throw soaked and drained aromatic wood chips or moistened fresh or dried herbs on the fire just before placing the fish on the grill.

Clean the grill rack well with a steel brush. Brush or spray a small amount of oil on the item to be grilled to prevent it from sticking to the grill.

If the fire dies out before the fish is fully cooked, finish the cooking in a conventional oven set to 425°F (220°C).

For indoor grilling with a grill pan, make sure the pan is hot before adding the food. This sometimes takes up to 10 minutes over high heat. Lower the heat if the pan starts to smoke. Oil the food rather than the pan. If desired, you can sear crisscross grill marks on the fish by turning it 90 degrees after a few minutes. Plan on cooking fish for 2 to 10 minutes, depending on the thickness.

BASIC RECIPES

Here are several recipes that anyone who cooks fish will find useful.

FISH STOCK

2½ lb (1.25 kg) fish bones, heads, and skin (see Note), well rinsed

1 large yellow onion, coarsely chopped

½ fennel bulb, trimmed and coarsely chopped

3 celery stalks, coarsely chopped

1 carrot, peeled and diced

1 leek, including tender green parts, chopped

6 cups (48 fl oz/1.5 l) water

2 cups (16 fl oz/500 ml) dry white wine

In a large saucepan, combine the fish parts, onion, fennel, celery, carrot, leek, water, and wine. Place over medium heat and bring gradually to a boil, skimming off foam as needed. Cover partially, reduce the heat to low, and simmer until the flesh starts to fall off the bones, about 25 minutes.

Line a sieve with cheesecloth (muslin) and place over a clean container. Strain the stock through the sieve. Use at once or let cool, cover tightly, and refrigerate for up to 3 days or freeze for up to 3 months. Makes about 2 qt (2 l).

Note: Ask your fishmonger to set aside some fish bones, sometimes called frames, or parts for you. Bones or parts from lean fish, such as cod, red snapper, flounder, and sole, are ideal. Avoid using bones from oily fish. Be sure the gills have been removed and the skin, if any, is free of scales.

BASIC BROILED FISH

1 fish fillet, 6–8 oz (185–250 g), or 1 fish steak, 6–8 oz (185–250 g), at room temperature

Dry white wine or water as needed

Adjust your oven rack so that the fish fillet or steak will be as near as possible to the broiler (grill)—about 4 inches (10 cm)—especially if it is a thin fillet. If necessary, use another pan upside down under the pan that will hold the fish.

Preheat the broiler to the hottest setting. If you are using an electric oven, it may take up to 10 minutes for the unit to get sufficiently hot.

Pour dry white wine or water to a depth of ⅛ inch (3 mm) into a shallow baking pan (don't use a broiler pan with slits in it or a rack) and lay the fish in the liquid. This will prevent the fish from sticking to the pan and, if using wine, will give it flavor. There is no need to turn the fish as it cooks.

Broil (grill) until the fish is golden brown and cooked through (pages 108–109).

A fillet or steak will cook in 2–10 minutes, depending on the thickness of the fish.

Serving Tip: Try serving a basic broiled fish fillet or steak atop a bed of sautéed julienned carrots, leeks, and fennel. Chopped fresh dill or other fresh herbs are also a nice addition.

RUBS, SAUCES, AND SALSAS

Use these recipes to dress up very simple broiled or grilled fish. See the listing of fish in the glossary (page 113) to determine which fish are suitable for broiling and grilling.

HOT-AND-SWEET CHILI RUB

2 tablespoons medium-hot chili powder

1 tablespoon sweet paprika

1 tablespoon firmly packed light brown sugar

½ teaspoon freshly ground pepper

¼ teaspoon coarse salt

In a small bowl, mix together all of the ingredients. Rub all over fish before cooking. Makes enough for 4 fish fillets or steaks.

Serving Tip: Use for all types of whole fish, fillets, and steaks.

SPICE-AND-HERB RUB

1½ tablespoons ground cumin

1 tablespoon dried thyme

1 teaspoon ground allspice

½ teaspoon ground nutmeg

¼ teaspoon freshly ground pepper

Pinch of cayenne pepper

In a small bowl, mix together all of the ingredients. Rub all over fish before cooking. Makes enough for 4 fish fillets or steaks.

Serving Tip: Use for firm, robust-tasting fish such as striped bass, tuna, or mahimahi.

PIQUANT SAUCE

2 tablespoons pine nuts

¼ cup (2 oz/60 g) unsalted butter

2 tablespoons olive oil

2 tablespoons fresh lemon juice

2 tablespoons minced fresh flat-leaf (Italian) parsley

Coarse salt and freshly ground pepper

In a small frying pan over medium heat, toast the pine nuts, stirring constantly, until golden. Pour onto a plate to cool.

In a small saucepan over medium-high heat, melt the butter with the oil. Add the lemon juice, swirl together, and add the parsley and toasted pine nuts. Season with salt and pepper. Drizzle over the fish at once. Makes 4 servings.

Serving Tip: Use for basic white-fleshed fish such as trout, sole, bass, and halibut.

THREE-PEPPER AND PINEAPPLE SALSA

½ cup (2½ oz/75 g) *each* finely diced red, green, and yellow bell peppers (capsicums)

1½ cups (9 oz/280 g) diced fresh or canned pineapple

1 tablespoon fresh lemon juice

1 teaspoon olive oil

Coarse salt and freshly ground pepper

In a bowl, mix together the peppers, pineapple, lemon juice, and olive oil. Season with salt and pepper. Makes 4 servings.

Serving Tip: Use for swordfish, mahimahi, or monkfish.

THAI-STYLE SAUCE

¼ cup (2 fl oz/60 ml) canola oil

3 cloves garlic, minced

2 tablespoons finely grated fresh ginger

1 stalk lemongrass, white part only, peeled and finely chopped

1 small jalapeño chile, minced

1 cup (8 fl oz/250 ml) sake

1 tablespoon dark Asian sesame oil

1 teaspoon fish sauce *(nam pla)*

Heat the oil in a small pan over medium-high heat. When hot, add the garlic and ginger. Cook for 1 minute, then add the lemongrass, chile, and sake. Bring to a boil, reduce the heat to medium-low, and simmer for 2 minutes. Pour into a bowl and whisk in the sesame oil and fish sauce. Serve warm or at room temperature drizzled over fish. Makes enough for 4 fish fillets or steaks.

Serving Tip: Use for mahimahi, Chilean sea bass, hailbut, sole, or fluke.

CORN, TOMATO, AND BACON SALSA

4 thick slices bacon

1 cup (6 oz/185 g) corn kernels, blanched for 2 minutes and drained

2 green (spring) onions, including tender green parts, finely sliced

1 tomato, diced

1 tablespoon fresh lemon juice

1 teaspoon olive oil

Coarse salt and freshly ground pepper

In a dry frying pan over medium heat, fry the bacon until crisp, about 6 minutes. Drain on paper towels and crumble. In a bowl, toss together the bacon and corn with the green onions, tomato, lemon juice, olive oil, and salt and pepper to taste. Makes 4 servings.

Serving Tip: Use for swordfish, shark, and cod.

ROASTED PEPPER AND TOMATO SALSA

2 red bell peppers (capsicums), roasted and peeled (page 74), then finely diced

2 tomatoes, finely diced

1 small red onion, finely diced

2 tablespoons minced fresh mint

1 tablespoon red wine vinegar

Coarse salt and freshly ground pepper

In a bowl, combine the peppers, tomatoes, onion, mint, and vinegar. Season with salt and pepper. Makes 4 servings.

Serving Tip: Use for striped bass, mackerel, and arctic char.

GLOSSARY

BROTH, CANNED Commercial broth and clam juice can be reliable, but they are seasoned with salt and other additives, such as monosodium glutamate. It is best to make your own stock so that you can season it to taste (see page 110).

CHIPOTLES EN ADOBO Chipotles are dried jalapeño chiles with a delicious strong smoky taste. They are commonly found canned in adobo sauce, a spicy tomato mixture made with paprika.

CHIVES These long, thin, dark green members of the onion family taste like a sweet onion. Using a chef's knife, cut them into pieces about ⅛ inch (3 mm) long, rather than mincing them. Some cooks use a pair of kitchen scissors to snip the chives, which is easier than chopping them.

EGG, RAW Eggs are sometimes used raw in dressings and other preparations. Raw eggs run a risk of being infected with salmonella or other bacteria, which can lead to food poisoning. This risk is of most concern to small children, older people, pregnant women, and anyone with a compromised immune system. If you have health and safety concerns, do not consume raw egg, or seek out a pasteurized egg product to replace it.

EGGS, SEPARATING When separating egg whites from yolks, start with cold eggs, which separate more easily than room-temperature eggs. Position 3 bowls side by side. Carefully crack each egg sharply on its equator on a flat surface, making a clean break; holding it over a bowl, pass the yolk back and forth between the shell halves and let the whites run into the bowl. Drop the yolk into the second bowl, and transfer the whites to the third bowl. Separate each additional egg over an empty bowl, for if any speck of yolk gets into the whites, the whites will not whip up properly. If a yolk breaks, start fresh with a new egg. You can also pour the yolk and whites into your clean, cupped hand, letting the whites run through your fingers into one of the bowls and depositing the yolk in another. Or, use an egg separator, a small bowl-shaped device with a depression made to hold the yolk while the white slips through. Let the separated eggs come to room temperature before using.

FISH

Anchovies: Harvested in waters worldwide, this small silver fish, popular in the Mediterranean, is often grilled. Most anchovies are preserved in salt or oil.

Arctic Char: A member of the salmon family, the arctic char is caught in the cold waters of Alaska, Canada, and Greenland and is also farmed. It has a light, delicate-tasting flesh and may replace salmon in any recipe, although it needs slightly more gentle handling.

Bass: Black sea bass, wild striped bass, farmed striped bass, white bass, and Chilean white sea bass all have fine, mild-tasting white flesh. Wild striped bass comes from the East Coast and is one of America's finest fish. It is best grilled, broiled, or roasted whole. Chilean white sea bass has somewhat fatty flesh that remains moist even if overcooked. Black sea bass, a delicate moist fish from the Atlantic, is often used for Asian preparations.

Bluefish: Caught nearly year-round along the East Coast, starting in the South in the spring, bluefish, a favorite with anglers, are delicious when fresh. Their dark flesh is suited to the grill and lightens when brushed with lime juice.

Carp: Looking like an oversized goldfish, carp grows in ponds and streams all over the United States. It has meaty flesh and is mixed with pike and whitefish to make gefilte fish.

Catfish: Large numbers of catfish are farmed in the southern United States, but the fish are found all over the world, mostly in freshwater. The flesh is sweet and moist and can be cooked any way you like, although panfried is best.

Cod: This lean, pearly white-fleshed fish is a favorite from the cold waters of the New England Atlantic coast. The smaller fish are often called scrod. Cod can be cooked by most methods, except on the grill, where it may flake. Add cod to a creamy soup or bake it with vegetables.

Dolphinfish: See Mahimahi.

Eel: Found in both fresh and salt water, eels have oily flesh that is fine when broiled, grilled, or stewed. Smoked eel is especially delicious.

Flounder: One of the Atlantic flatfish often sold as sole, flounder have delicate white flesh and cook quickly.

Fluke: Like flounder, flukes are often called sole. They are available from the Atlantic in abundance during summer.

Grouper: A large family of fish from the southern Atlantic and the cold Pacific, groupers have somewhat coarse flesh that resembles red snapper and can be grilled, broiled, or baked.

Haddock: Mild flavored and lean, haddock is part of the cod family and is from the Atlantic. They can be treated in the same way as cod.

Halibut: Large flatfish from the cold waters of the Atlantic and Pacific, halibut's firm, white flesh is very versatile. It is as delicious with plenty of spice as it is with a buttery hollandaise sauce.

Herring: These slightly oily fish come from the Atlantic and Pacific and can be grilled or broiled. When small herring are in season, they are sold as sardines.

Lingcod: Also called green cod, this lean fish is caught in Alaskan waters and down to British Columbia. Cook it like cod.

Mackerel: This oily fish is superb when freshly caught from the Atlantic in the spring and autumn. It is perfect for grilling or broiling.

Mahimahi: Also known as dolphinfish, mahimahi is found in warm waters worldwide. It is a firm fish and therefore suitable for the grill. It can also be broiled or baked.

Monkfish: Monkfish, fished from the northern Atlantic, has an ugly appearance that is more than compensated for by its firm, pearly white meat. Also known as goosefish, it absorbs flavors well and can be braised with tomatoes.

Perch: This lean, mild freshwater fish may be cooked by any method.

Pike: A freshwater fish with mild-tasting, sweet, lean flesh, pike is exceptionally bony. Grill, broil, or bake it.

Pompano: Fished from the Atlantic off Florida and also from the Gulf of Mexico, this pretty fish is excellent cooked whole, baked, or broiled.

Redfish: A lean fish from the south-eastern coast of America and the Gulf of Mexico, redfish is also called drum. Serve it broiled, grilled, or blackened.

Rockfish: Numerous species of rockfish are found worldwide. They resemble the snapper and are often erroneously called red snapper, particularly on the West Coast, where they are fished from the Pacific. The flesh is mild and white and can be broiled, fried, or baked.

Salmon: Five species of salmon come from the West Coast and one comes from the Atlantic, where the wild salmon have been all but fished out. Norway, Canada, the United States, Ireland, and Scotland farm Atlantic salmon. They are excellent, although rather oily. Wild salmon—chinook (king), chum, coho, pink, and sockeye from the West Coast—are caught seasonally from late spring through summer. Salmon can be cooked by any method, in steaks, fillets, medaillons, or whole.

Sand Dab: A sweet and lean flatfish from the Pacific ocean. Treat sand dab as a flounder or sole.

Sardine: A small, silvery, moderately oily fish from the Atlantic and Pacific that can be cooked by any method. Larger sardines from the Mediterranean are good grilled or broiled. Many sardines are canned.

Shad: This oily freshwater fish from the Atlantic has mild, sweet flesh and is best broiled. Briefly sautéed shad roe, or eggs, is a springtime favorite.

Shark: A family of lean, meaty fish that are caught worldwide. Most commonly eaten are the shortfin mako, soupfin, black tip, and spiny dogfish varieties. Cook shark steaks by any method.

Skate: Found in waters worldwide, skate, also called ray, has prickly skin and white, lean flesh. We eat the wings of the skate, which are skinned before being broiled, fried, or grilled. See page 49.

Smelt: These small, slender fish live in the Atlantic and Pacific but spawn in rivers. Sweet and lean, they are good split and then fried, grilled, or broiled.

Snapper: A family of tender but firm, lean, mild fish from the warm waters of the Atlantic. The American red snapper and yellowtail snapper are the most popular varieties. Red snapper is also the name given to the Pacific rockfish. It can be cooked by any method.

Sole: The name given to many flatfish that have lean, sweet flesh. Dover, lemon, gray, petrale, and rex are some of the common sole varieties. They are fished in the cold waters of the Atlantic and Pacific. Sauté, poach, or fry the delicate fillets with extra care.

Swordfish: This giant of a fish, with a long swordlike snout, is found in the warmer oceans of the world. Always sold as a chunk or steak, the flesh is lean and moist when cooked.

Tilefish: Lean, mild Atlantic fish found from Cape Cod down to Mexico. Usually filleted or cut into steaks, they can be cooked by any method.

Trout: A delicate, somewhat oily fresh-water fish that is primarily farmed in Idaho but found everywhere. They come to the market already boned (head left on) weighing 6 to 10 ounces (185 to 315 g) each, for an ample single portion. Trout can be fried, grilled, broiled, or braised.

Tuna: A large torpedo-shaped fish from moderately warm waters around the world, the tuna, a member of the mackerel family, is cut into four loins when marketed. Use only sashimi-quality tuna for raw preparations such as sushi, ceviche, or tuna tartare. Yellowfin tuna is a commonly found variety. Other tuna are bluefin (the most precious), bigeye, albacore, skipjack, and bonito.

Weakfish: Also known as sea trout, weakfish are found in the Atlantic most of the year. They have lean and delicate flesh. Handled with care, they can be cooked by any method.

Whitefish: From cold lakes and streams, whitefish is a sweet, moderately oily fish. It is excellent roasted whole and is also available smoked. When smoked, the smaller fish are called chubs.

FLESH SIDE VS. SKIN SIDE Fillets of fish are often skinned before purchase. (Thin skin is edible, so this is not absolutely necessary.) The skinned side usually appears slightly streaked, with thin white remnants of the skin still showing. Score this side when sautéing, so that the fillet will not curl up. The flesh side is the more attractive one. Be sure to cook the flesh side first, and to present it facing up in the finished dish.

NONALUMINUM Selecting cookware made from a nonreactive material such as stainless steel, enamel, or glass is important when cooking with acidic ingredients such as citrus juice, vinegar, wine, tomatoes, and most vegetables. Cookware made with materials such as aluminum (and, to a lesser degree, cast iron or unlined copper) will react with acidic ingredients and may impart a metallic taste and grayish color.

SALT, COARSE Many of the recipes in this book call for coarse salt. Kosher salt is a good choice. Made by compressing granular salt, it has coarse grains and no additives. Not as salty as table salt, it can be used more liberally. Sea salt is also available in coarse grains.

SKIN SIDE See Flesh Side vs. Skin Side.

SPATULAS For cooking a large fillet or whole fish, you will need 2 metal spatulas each about 3 inches (7.5 cm) wide and 8 inches (20 cm) long with sturdy wooden handles. One spatula will work for smaller fillets and steaks.

THERMOMETER, INSTANT-READ A handy tool for testing the doneness of a fish. To test, toward the end of cooking, insert the thermometer into the thickest part of the fish away from the bone (bone conducts heat). Within 30 seconds you will get a correct reading (140°F/60°C indicates fully cooked for fish).

ZEST The zest is the colored portion of the peel of a citrus fruit without the bitter white pith. To zest a lemon, lime, or orange, use the fine rasps on a hand-held grater, or use a zester, a metal blade with 4 to 6 sharp-edged holes mounted on a short handle that allows the removal of the zest in long, wispy strips.

INDEX

SIMON & SCHUSTER SOURCE
A Division of Simon & Schuster Inc.
Rockefeller Center
1230 Avenue of the Americas
New York, NY 10020

WILLIAMS-SONOMA
Founder and Vice-Chairman: Chuck Williams
Book Buyer: Cecilia Michaelis

WELDON OWEN INC.
Chief Executive Officer: John Owen
President: Terry Newell
Chief Operating Officer: Larry Partington
Vice President, International Sales: Stuart Laurence
Creative Director: Gaye Allen
Series Editor: Sarah Putman Clegg
Associate Editor: Heather Belt
Production Manager: Chris Hemesath
Photograph Editor: Lisa Lee

Weldon Owen wishes to thank the following
people for their generous assistance and support in
producing this book: Copy Editor Carolyn Miller;
Consulting Editors Sharon Silva and Norman Kolpas;
Designer Douglas Chalk; Food Stylist George Dolese;
Photographer's Assistant Noriko Akiyama; Associate
Food Stylist Leslie Busch; Assistant Food Stylist
Elisabet der Nederlanden; Assistant Photograph
Editor Kris Ellis; Proofreaders Desne Ahlers and
Carrie Bradley; Indexer Ken DellaPenta; and
Production Designer Joan Olson.

Williams-Sonoma Collection *Fish* was
conceived and produced by Weldon Owen Inc.,
814 Montgomery Street, San Francisco,
California 94133, in collaboration with
Williams-Sonoma, 3250 Van Ness Avenue,
San Francisco, California 94109.

A Weldon Owen Production
Copyright © 2002 by Weldon Owen Inc. and
Williams-Sonoma Inc.

Set in Trajan, Utopia, and Vectora.

Color separations by Bright Arts Graphics
Singapore (Pte.) Ltd.
Printed and bound in Singapore by Tien Wah
Press (Pte.) Ltd.

For information about special discounts for
bulk purchases, please contact Simon & Schuster
Special Sales: 1-800-456-6798 or
business@simonandschuster.com

First printed in 2002.

10 9 8 7 6 5 4 3 2

Library of Congress Cataloging-in-Publication Data

King, Shirley.
 Fish / recipes and text, Shirley King ; general
editor, Chuck Williams ; photographs, Noel
Barnhurst.
    p. cm. — (Williams-Sonoma collection)
 1. Cookery (Fish) I. Williams, Chuck. II. Title.
III. Williams-Sonoma collection (New York, N.Y.)

TX747 .K5197 2002
641.6'92—dc21

                              2001042901
ISBN 0-7432-2640-2

A NOTE ON WEIGHTS AND MEASURES

All recipes include customary U.S. and metric measurements. Metric conversions are based on
a standard developed for these books and have been rounded off. Actual weights may vary.